GIGWORKER

GIGWORKER

INDEPENDENT WORK AND
THE STATE OF THE GIG ECONOMY

BRETT HELLING

LIONCREST
PUBLISHING

GIGWORKER

Independent Work and the State of the Gig Economy

ISBN   978-1-5445-0775-0 *Paperback*

978-1-5445-0776-7 *Ebook*

For my mom and dad, who have been two of
my biggest supporters my entire life.

CONTENTS

INTRODUCTION

Sam looks away from his computer screen and sighs.

Another day doing the same thing, he thinks to himself. He has been sitting at this desk working for the same accounting firm for ten years now.

I never wanted to be a slave to the clock, yet here I am.

He clocks in every Monday at eight o'clock in the morning and clocks out at five o'clock in the evening and then repeats that until Friday. He looks forward to each weekend to get away from the drudgery.

A talented software developer, Sam loves solving problems with code, but he's written enough accounting software to last him a lifetime. Even so, he doesn't feel any sense of pride or personal accomplishment. He so far hasn't created something *he* wanted. He only created things for his employer.

What have I really accomplished over the past ten years? Sam asks himself. *What have I done for myself?*

When he first started in his role at his company, he had his eyes set on moving up the ladder. He put in countless hours in the hopes of being promoted to the head of his department. He wanted to be the boss. But it's been ten years, and that hasn't happened, despite putting in the time, effort, and sacrifice proving himself to be a committed and valuable employee. And with recent changes to the company structure, it doesn't look like there's any room for upward growth. He's grown tired of the office politics and interpersonal drama. He's burnt out and uninspired.

I'm talented. I'm a hard worker, Sam thinks to himself. *I'm too good for this place.*

He'd like to develop and work on his own projects, but he never seems to have the time or energy to spend with his family. He daydreams about traveling with his wife in early retirement but can't see how he's ever going to leave his job. He feels stuck, frustrated, and alone.

I can't just leave a steady job with good pay and benefits. But

I'm also miserable. This job is less than ideal for the lifestyle I want.

People keep telling him he has options, that he's not limited. "You're a smart person," they say. "Go out and do your own thing." They say he could join the gig economy, become a freelancer, and do contract work, but Sam doesn't take them seriously. The gig economy doesn't seem like the right place for him. Isn't it just Uber and Airbnb? He's a programmer, not a cabbie or a landlord.

If Sam were to investigate further, however, he'd find there are many ways to use his skills in the gig economy, but like many people, he has a limited view of what gig work means today. Most people never look beyond ridesharing and vacation rentals. The big names in gig work, like Uber, Airbnb, and Lyft, make the most noise, so they're top of mind, but the gig economy is much more than just app-based gigs. If you take a step back and survey the landscape of gig work, you'll discover a vast world of options—from professions like graphic design and software development to services like pet sitting and package delivery.

Sam can still do what he's doing now—what he's good at—but instead, work as an independent contractor. He can be a consultant and have multiple clients. He can make his own schedule. He can charge an hourly rate that values his time and his talents.

And that's the real beauty of gig work. He can do what he's doing now, on his own time, unlocking exactly what he wants: freedom and flexibility.

A VAST ARRAY OF OPPORTUNITIES

Once people start researching today's gig economy, they often discover that their biggest problem isn't a lack of opportunities but the difficulty in choosing from the wealth of possibilities available to them. The sheer number of options can be overwhelming.

Whether they're skeptical or overwhelmed, they feel stuck, unable to move forward. Worse, there doesn't seem to be anybody around who can help them figure it all out. They feel alone.

The reality is that they're far from alone—over fifty-seven million people freelanced in 2018[1], and that number is growing. The gig landscape is full of opportunity; it's vast, varied, and not difficult to navigate if you have the right information. I wrote this book and created the Gigworker. com website to dispel these myths and make it easy for workers in all professions to understand the ins and outs of independent work, so they can skillfully explore their options.

---

1   Freelancing in America: 2018, Upwork and Freelancer's Union report, Edelman Intelligence, October 2018

And the gig economy is growing, which isn't surprising. Who wouldn't want to work for themselves? Who wouldn't want to make their own hours and be in charge of their own time? Who wouldn't want their own freedom and flexibility? You can work your own schedule. You call the shots. You have the flexibility to work when you want to, and you have the freedom to do whatever else might motivate you.

Do you want to go for a five-mile hike in the middle of the day when the sun is shining, the air is crisp, and the hiking conditions are just right?

Do you want to travel to a remote island in the Caribbean to scuba dive for weeks on end yet still have the ability to work from a laptop on the beach in between dives?

Do you want to learn how to fly a helicopter, taking flight courses mid-week in the middle of the day?

Do you want to spend more time with your kids, aging parents, family, or friends?

The gig economy unlocks all of that for you—and more. You can shamelessly live life on your own terms.

Before I jumped into the gig economy, I constantly asked myself those types of questions and answered them with phrases like, "That'd be the life." Nowadays, I answer them while looking at my calendar, saying, "When and where?"

WHAT'S IN THIS BOOK?

The gig economy is a big scary place with many options. At first glance, if you don't know what you're doing, you don't know which option is best for you. You might panic when you start out, but you don't have to because millions of people have done this already. Countless people have been in your shoes, and you can learn from them. After all, you don't have to reinvent the wheel to succeed.

I wrote this book to draw on the knowledge gained by millions of gig workers over the past decade, so you don't have to figure it out from scratch.

In these pages, I offer you a hand up by eliminating much of the guesswork involved in joining the gig economy. I want you to have as much information at your fingertips as possible, so you know you're not alone, and you know what next steps to take right now. By reading this book, you can develop a clearer view of the broad landscape of gig work available today and a sense of the opportunities to come.

What we'll cover:

- How the gig economy evolved.

- What gig work looks like today.
- Some myths and realities.
- Opportunities and risks in the gig economy.
- How to get started.
- How to maximize your success.
- How to avoid pitfalls and manage obstacles.
- The experiences of gig workers who have thrived.
- What's next for the gig economy.

WHY SHOULD YOU LISTEN TO ME?

I'm a huge champion of the gig economy today, but I started out just like Sam. I accepted the status quo of going to college, majoring in something that would eventually turn into a career, and then working in that career for decades. I fell for pursuing each step of the so-called "career path" that we're taught to pursue our entire lives. In college, if you had asked me what my future would look like, I'd tell you I'd find a good-paying Monday-through-Friday job in the corporate world with excellent benefits where I'd grind it out just like everybody else.

That's what we're all supposed to do, right?

In college, I interned at a financial services company on the administrative side of things. I also interned in the IT department of a local hospital. While both of these could have been long-term careers for me, I saw what effect it had on those working around me. They were unhappy with their careers, and that then bled into their personal lives—and boy, did they complain about everything and let that be known in the workplace. They were absolutely miserable, and they weren't shy about admitting it.

After a while, those negative vibes started rubbing off on me. I started to grow bitter, too. These jobs served their purpose of paying the bills, but they didn't excite me. And although they offered stability and security, the environments were toxic. Everyone was so negative, which was incredibly hard for me to stomach because I'm such a positive person. I try to see the good in everything, but the toxic environment eventually started to consume me.

Luckily, I was born with an innate desire to build things from the ground up. I am naturally attracted to building something from nothing, which excites and motivates me. It's almost like a game that I can't get enough of. Despite me pursuing a "long-term career" throughout college, I also worked a variety of gigs and side projects—not so much because I needed the money, but because that innate desire to build something out of scratch continually knocked on my door.

While interning at the financial company, for example, I started an online bookstore for my fellow college students. College books are horrendously expensive, and I quickly grew tired of watching the campus bookstore gouge students with high purchase and low resale prices. When students resold the books back to the school bookstore after their courses ended, they didn't pocket even half of what they initially paid just a few months prior at the start of the semester. It was a predatory business practice masquerading as a helpful service to the students. Unfortunately, many students, especially the younger ones, didn't know any better and played into the ruse.

Seeing an opportunity to build something new, I decided to change that, so I built an online bookstore to buy back books from students on local college campuses. My twin brother had been flipping books for a few months before I started and was kind enough to let me in on the action, too. I took my venture online and automated much of the process.

I gave students a bigger return for their used college textbooks and then sold them online for even more. And although the profit margins were good, I reveled in creating something from scratch that was a win-win for everyone involved.

When I interned in IT at the hospital, a few other interns and I started mining bitcoin, among other cryptocurrencies, because we thought it was an interesting concept that had the potential to take off into something bigger than it was at the time. I even went so far as to lease computing power from a server farm in Iceland since the electricity there was so much cheaper than mining them stateside. At the time, my unhappy middle-aged coworkers incessantly made fun of us for playing with "fake money," but we cut out the noise and persisted. This was before bitcoin exploded in 2017, reaching all-time highs—which is when I sold my share and exited the market. Guess who had the last laugh?

In 2015, I even tried my hand at aerial videography. I bought a massive, four-foot-wide drone with a cinema-grade camera with the intention of creating stunning aerial videos for businesses. Unfortunately, there were a lot of regulations with drones at the time—which I learned the hard way. On one project for a client, I accidentally flew my drone too close to a police helicopter. Next thing I knew, the police showed up in squad cars. Regardless of the retractable landing gear, standalone gimbal-stabilized 4k camera, lightweight carbon fiber body frame, and state-of-the-art collision avoidance system, the police did not think the setup was nearly as cool as I did, and they shut down my shoot. Nerding out on technology has a time and a place. Needless to say, I learned very quickly that when the police show up to your video shoot, that is neither the time nor the place to nerd out.

Shortly thereafter, Uber entered the field. I'll admit I thought Uber was a pretty strange concept when it first rolled into my city. I wasn't sure people would feel comfortable hopping into my personal vehicle and paying for a ride, but I was intrigued, so I jumped in with both feet and signed up to become a driver. After getting approved, which took just hours, I very quickly realized that I had absolutely no idea what I was doing; the training I received via two three-minute videos supplied by Uber didn't give me much to go on. I didn't know where to go to pick people up or when, so I just started aimlessly driving my 2011 Acura TL Type-S around town, guessing until I figured it out. Soon, I came to love the freedom, independence, and growth potential of this kind of work almost as much as the money and the stories that came with the gig.

By the end of my first week, I realized there were millions of other drivers out there who loved it, too. But because Uber's training was so basic, I saw a need to create a website to give fellow drivers the resources needed to survive and thrive. I thus created what is now Ridester.com, a website dedicated to collecting and sharing the most helpful and useful information about the rideshare world in one place.

At first, when I started the site, I pretty much just shared stories about what I did that worked for me. Then I expanded into providing information about driver promotions, which led to information about passenger promotions, which eventually led to me publishing complete guides and evergreen content about the industry as a whole, for both riders and drivers. Soon, the website was full of tips, tricks, helpful guides for driving, and personal anecdotes—and I was spending a lot more time on building the website than I was driving.

People clearly needed this information—within two years, Ridester grew from two hundred thousand unique visitors per month to 1.5 million—but it only covered a small segment of the gig economy, which seemed poised to become a much bigger beast. Little did I know at the time what the gig economy would become just a few years later.

Unfortunately, I didn't spend the time Ridester.com needed for it to grow because I was still a student *and* interning not just for the IT department at the hospital but also for my dad's company. In fact, while I was building Ridester, my dad asked me to build a site for his company, too. Now, mind you, I didn't go to school for web development, so I was learning how to build sites on my own. I learned quickly, though, and soon enough, I was approached by several other people and companies, asking me to create a site of their own.

Even though Ridester was growing and bringing in some revenue through Uber and Lyft's referral programs and ads, and despite making some extra cash building sites, it wasn't enough for me to fully commit to the gig economy.

Upon graduating from college in December 2013, I was hit

with a quarter-life crisis. I had studied marketing, management, and entrepreneurship in school, but I had no idea what I wanted to do. My work experiences shaped my formative years in my career, but they didn't provide enough clarity. Did I want to be secure and pursue a job working for someone else? Or did I want to risk it all and earn money by building websites?

On one hand, I knew working in an office environment wasn't ideal. I wouldn't do well in the all-too-common negative and toxic environments that I had previously experienced. And yet, on the other hand, I was nervous about not getting enough web design clients to fully support myself as a freelancer.

As I contemplated my next steps, a job opened up at my dad's event planning company. After a little discussion, we decided that I might be a good fit. Since the job sounded super fun—and because it provided an immediate answer to my quarter-life crisis—I accepted.

In January 2014, I joined my father's event planning company full time, planning and producing huge corporate events for some of the largest companies in the United States. But we did much more than what you might think about when hearing "corporate events." Attendees and clients expected a show, so we gave them one, with cutting-edge technology like projection mapping and digital graphics. Instead of just renting microphones and small screens like you see at most conferences, we'd run massive videos on 100-foot-wide screens. Or we'd connect a bunch of TVs and program them to run simultaneously for a unique visual experience. Or we'd spend six months figuring out how to project dynamic, custom-made presentations onto a 120-foot-wide stage. We'd create live presentations on 3D surfaces with a variety of other pieces that interacted with one another. In a word, what we did was badass. This stuff didn't just impress the audience; it blew their minds.

I was constantly traveling for shows, spending weeks at a time at various locations around the country. We were doing a minimum of twenty shows a year, so as soon as one ended, we'd jump straight into another. My friends would call me and ask where I was; oftentimes, I couldn't even remember what city I was in because the sheer number of trips blended together. As a recent college graduate, I was living the dream: fortunate enough to be seeing much of the world while doing a job I loved.

Due to the uniqueness of the experiences we were creating, the run-up to each event required weeks of preparation, in addition to the many months spent meticulously planning each experience. My boss and I were in charge of ensuring that the technology worked for each one. We'd spend days packing up our gear, traveling, and unpacking. In between the shows, I worked on developing technology we had never used before in a live show environment, so there was a lot of learning, experimenting, and testing. Sometimes things wouldn't work as we expected, but since "no" is not a good option in any situation involving clients, we would figure out a way to make them work, no matter what. This sometimes involved staying up all night until we got things working properly.

The nature of the work forced us to adhere to deadlines that were critical to our success. As a corporate event planning and production company, it wasn't like we could push things off to the next week, let alone the next day. I felt proud of my responsibilities—if I didn't do them, nobody else would, and not only would the event fail, but I would let everyone in the company down.

We created experiences people would never forget, and I reveled in being part of that. The company work was cool but also very intense. It taught me the value of hard work, prioritization of tasks, and resilience when things got tough. However, I had a problem that I couldn't seem to work through.

Between everything I had going on at work, with my additional side hustles and romantic relationships, I had zero personal time. To top things off, I was still aggressively building Ridester on the side. I slept maybe four hours a night at the most. Even though I bore sole responsibility for taking on far more than I could handle, I still grew frustrated. The many different things I'd committed to were taking time away from implementing the various improvements I thought up for Ridester. Everything I did for Ridester at the time seemed rushed and sloppy if I even had the chance to work on it at all.

Finding a proper balance was incredibly taxing—emotionally, physically, and mentally. With so much to do at all times, my healthy habits started to drop off the wayside. I stopped working out. I constantly ate fast food because it was convenient. I gained a surprising amount of weight and began to feel sluggish and depressed.

One day, things came to a head as I stared at my packed calendar. It seemed like I would never get a break. That day, my brother came over to my house to take me to dinner, but he found me crying in my bedroom closet, completely overwhelmed. My commitments were never-ending, and I was slowly breaking myself down. I was exhausted. My mental well-being was suffering. I wasn't taking care of myself. My relationships with others, including my girlfriend at the time, greatly suffered.

Something had to give. I had a gut feeling that I could excel at independent work on my own, but like Sam and millions of others, I was reluctant to make the leap from a conventional full-time job to gig work. It was doubly hard for me because leaving my full-time job meant leaving my father's company. I dreaded having that conversation with him. I felt like I was letting him down. I enjoyed nothing more than working with him, and I knew he liked working with me as well. Some of the best memories we've shared were in the middle of those shows, staying up all night together to figure out a problem, or meeting a deadline for the next day. Although the schedule was tough, that job provided me with some of the most fulfilling experiences of my life.

Would he be disappointed? Would the company suffer? Would they be able to find someone to replace me? If I was so stressed, how would me leaving and having to train a replacement among the chaos impact my coworkers?

As worried as I was, I had to face some hard truths. I had seen what full-time positions had done to others. I saw it during my internships, I saw it with friends after college, and I suffered through it myself when I overcommitted to everything. Close friends had dreams of starting their own business but never made the jump to commit to actually bring their ideas to life. They then got married, had kids, and had to eventually settle for being in a position and career that really wasn't their dream or passion. I didn't want that for myself, so I swallowed any uneasy feelings and was honest with my dad. As much as I loved working in the family business, deep down, I knew I had to venture out on my own, take a risk, and try my hand at building something myself—something of my own creation.

In the end, he understood, but leaving was still scary. I had been making some money with Ridester but leaving my father's company meant I had to hustle and make a lot more. Fortunately, I joined a new economy that was growing fast.

With time, I successfully implemented a handful of my ideas and monetized Ridester.com to a point where the site made more than it ever had before. It wasn't easy, but my dedication and hard work paid off, and I began to see the power of being self-employed.

More importantly, I achieved the ultimate goal: freedom and flexibility.

Today, not only am I thriving in the gig economy, I hire other gig workers. Throughout the year, I employ between ten to twenty gig workers to help me bring value to others. I still run Ridester.com and am continually adding to and expanding the information and resources available on Gigworker.com. I've also recently acquired Bloggingtips.com, a comprehensive online resource that teaches aspiring bloggers how to start, build, grow, and monetize a blog every step of the way.

Although the gig economy has been around for decades,

it's really on the brink of exploding—especially in light of COVID-19 (more on that later). Gigworker.com, although ready for you to visit today, is a constant work in progress. I see a lot of parallels between Ridester.com and Gigworker. com. What Ridester was for new Uber and Lyft drivers years ago is what I hope Gigworker will become to those in the gig economy.

ARE YOU READY TO MAKE A CHANGE?

This book will help you if you're curious about the gig economy, whether you're currently part of it or not. We'll go broad, considering the societal and economic trends unfolding now, and we'll also go deep, offering specific tools and strategies you can use to make the most of this movement. In other words, I'll share a lot of information, but I'm not going to just dump it on you and leave you to figure out what to do with it. My intent is to set you up for success.

This book is for you if you are:

- Curious about the growing gig economy.
- A college graduate who needs to pay your bills.
- Established in your career but frustrated because you have reached a dead end.
- Sick of the nine-to-five corporate grind.
- Missing out on the life you want outside of work.

- Thinking about retirement and realizing you'll need to supplement your savings.
- Already in the gig economy but have yet to reach your goals.
- Willing to put in the time, make the mind shift, and do the work.
- Or anywhere in between!

If you see yourself anywhere on this list, I invite you to join me in exploring the wide-open world of independent work in the following pages and on my website Gigworker.com.

CHAPTER ONE

EVOLUTION OF THE GIG

The gig economy feels like a modern phenomenon, but it didn't just materialize out of thin air. "Gigs" have been around since even before jazz musicians started using the word to describe their performances. If we consider gig work to be any part-time, freelance work, we can see that all kinds of people have been taking all kinds of gigs for a very long time.

In the 1930s, for instance, the Great Depression forced many farmers to sell their land and become migrant farmworkers, moving from farm to farm to help with the annual harvest. Temporary jobs became popular in the mid-1940s, with agencies like Russell Kelly Office Services and Manpower, Inc. placing workers in various gigs on an as-needed basis. These short-term gigs allowed mothers to help provide for the family, introducing a new balance of staying at home with their kids *and* working.

After that, society's attitudes about work changed dramatically. Traditional salaried jobs, once the default option for most workers, were no longer the only game in town. Anyone looking for work, and anyone hiring, now had to consider contract work—gig work—as a given and accepted part of the business landscape.

INITIAL SURGE

Throughout the 1990s, independent work became even more accessible through online classified ads on boards such as Craigslist, and through exchanges on websites such as Elance and oDesk (now Upwork), where employers advertise their needs and workers respond. This kind of crowdsourcing brought visibility to independent, remote workers and gave employers reliable access to an ever-growing global talent pool. Soon, there were crowdsourcing sites for all types of work, including the simple, repetitive tasks on sites like Amazon's Mechanical Turk, that offered as little as 10 cents per task. By 1995, 10 percent of Americans worked in alternative, or gig, employment.[2]

During the dot com boom, we saw a lot of people throwing money at new internet companies simply because they

2   https://www.nber.org/papers/w22667.

sounded interesting or promised revolutionary disruption. There was a general FOMO (fear of missing out) mentality that I liken to what North America saw during the California Gold Rush of 1848. When gold was first discovered in California, a wave of FOMO swept the minds of thousands of men who left their wives and homes in search of vast fortunes. In the late 1990s, that same mentality swept investors to invest in various internet companies, thinking the return would be highly profitable. And since the internet was a new phenomenon, people feared missing out on this new technology that was sure to take over. Some companies, like PayPal, did alright, but most ended up failing by 2002.

I see the same thing happening today with startups, especially those in the gig economy. SoftBank is an example of a company that suffered from FOMO as they entered the gig economy. SoftBank threw a ton of money at gig employers, like WeWork and Uber, for example. Unfortunately, internal mismanagement within some of those companies caused SoftBank to lose nearly $4.5 billion with WeWork and $5.2 billion with Uber[3].

Gig work entered the mainstream steadily at first, chugging along but moving slowly compared to what would happen in the early 2000s. A decade into the new century, the gig

3   https://www.bloomberg.com/news/articles/2020-05-18/
    softbank-vision-fund-books-17-7-billion-loss-on-wework-uber.

economy became more of a runaway train, moving much faster than most people had anticipated.

How fast? This fast:[4]

- Airbnb, founded in 2009 by roommates hoping to make the rent by taking on part-time boarders, began with 2,500 listings. By the beginning of 2012, the company boasted over one hundred thousand listings. By 2018, they were worth $38 million.
- TaskRabbit, created in 2008 as a site for hiring people to run errands and do simple chores, quickly grew to cover nearly any task, from repairs to wake-up calls. By 2017, sixty thousand taskers offered their services through the platform. The company was eventually purchased by Ikea.
- In 2010, when two entrepreneurs noticed how hard it was to find a reliable and inexpensive ride, especially in bad weather, they designed an app called Uber that let users request a ride with the tap of a button. Five years later, Uber drivers had accepted 1 billion rides, and the company is now one of the world's most popular and valuable transportation and logistics companies.
- Lyft, Uber's main competitor in ridesharing, served 1.56 million annual riders in 2013 and an astounding 265 million in 2017.

---

4   Jessup, History of the Gig Economy, October 23, 2018, https://online.jessup.edu/blog/business/history-of-the-gig-economy/.

HOW DID THEY GROW SO FAST?

How did all these companies manage to grow despite the financial recession of 2008-2009? There are a couple of reasons: They adopted a growth mindset and took big risks in order to capture as much market share as possible, despite costs, and they had technology on their side.

GROWTH MINDSET

While the financial world seemingly crashed around them in 2008, most gig companies adopted and made decisions that revolved around a growth mindset as opposed to a short-term strategic one. Instead of worrying about how they would make money right off the bat (strategic), they wanted to capture as much of the market share as possible (growth). At the time, that growth mindset was far more important to them than profits alone. Once they successfully captured enough market share, they would figure out the operational efficiencies that would allow them to be profitable at a later time.

In order to capture the market, these various gig companies ran incredibly aggressive affiliate and referral programs, which offered huge incentives.

Rideshare companies experienced astonishing, unheard-of growth by leveraging their rider and driver bases to promote their affiliate programs among their friends and family. Uber, for example, gave out $1,000 cash bonuses to anyone who successfully recruited other drivers that had previous Lyft experience. This was pivotal. If I recruited an existing Lyft driver to switch rideshare services to drive with Uber, not only would I get the $1,000, but the driver I recruited would get $1,000, too. That's a lot of money for a new company.

When you think about it, Uber's affiliate program was pretty savage; they shelled out a total of $2,000 just to poach each driver from their competitor. My friend Jonnie made tens of thousands of dollars in just one month by taking Lyft rides and converting the drivers to Uber. It was a two-way incentive—and it worked.

This became one of my revenue streams as well. Instead of monetizing Ridester.com through pay-per-click ads alone, I also used the site to educate drivers about these incentives. I kept tabs on each of the rideshare companies' affiliate programs and wrote articles about them. I then encouraged my readers to click the links on my pages to sign up to be a driver, and when they did, we would each get a payout from the programs. With each successful sign-up, I would get up to $1,000, sometimes even more. These affiliate programs were a strong source of income for me for several years—until the companies offering them put a global limit on how much any one person could make on their programs. That's why it's important to never put all your eggs in one basket; more on this later.

Airbnb, TaskRabbit, Postmates, Instacart, and DoorDash ran similar programs, although not as lucrative (see box). If you referred a friend on TaskRabbit, for example, you and that friend would both get $50 credit added to your account. I viewed these programs as grassroots guerilla marketing. People would invite their friends and family members in order to capitalize on the incentives. By doing so, these companies increased their market share and rapidly grew—even during a recession. Pretty brilliant, really.

PREVIOUSLY OFFERED AFFILIATE COMMISSIONS

Low-end Labor Platforms:

- Uber: Up to $1,000 for new driver referrals, up to $20 for new rider referrals.
- Lyft: $600 for new driver referrals, $20 for new rider referrals.
- DoorDash: $50 for new driver referrals.
- Postmates: $250 for new driver referrals, $50 for new customer referrals.
- Instacart: $5 for each shopper who applied, $50 for each one that was approved to shop.
- Taskrabbit: $50 in credit for new referrals.

Skilled Labor Platforms:

- Toptal: refer a company to Toptal and receive $2,000 when they become a paying client.

Property Rental Platforms:

- Airbnb: $200 for new host referrals.

Training Platforms:

- LinkedIn Learning: $10 per trial sign-up.

All of that growth, however, came at an expense. The companies that grew during the recession took billions of dollars in losses in order to capture as much market share as possible. They wanted to become a household name before they achieved profitability—and it paid off. Uber's founder, Travis Kalanick, didn't mind not making money at first. He wanted drivers, and he wanted riders. And he successfully acquired them both with Uber's lucrative affiliate incentives.

Uber has since become much more than just a rideshare service. Even as they were still figuring out the unit economics of giving rides, they rolled out new services—what they call "other bets"—like Uber Eats, a food delivery service; Uber Freight, which connects truck drivers with shippers, much in the same way the company's ride-hailing app pairs drivers with those looking for a ride; and new mobility ventures like their Jump-branded electric bikes and scooters. Most recently, they've created a platform that connects on-demand workers with short-term work, like restaurant shifts. Although Travis is no longer the CEO of Uber, the company continues to operate under the growth model.

This constant forward momentum has allowed Uber to amass a large war chest, raise more money, and expand their reach. Uber is everywhere and not going away any time soon.

By 2018, Uber had ninety-one million monthly active platform consumers, bringing in a revenue of $11.3 billion. Over 80 percent of this revenue was from its ridesharing products, which totaled revenue of $9.2 billion. Over fifteen million people used Uber Eats in the last quarter of 2018, resulting in gross bookings of $2.6 billion. Uber Freight brought in $125 million in revenue for the quarter ending on December 31, 2018. Uber's gross bookings totaled $41.5 billion in 2018 (Uber defines gross bookings as the total dollar value, including any applicable taxes, tolls, and fees, of service without any adjustment).[5]

By the end of 2019, Travis switched gears to another kind of shareable market known as "ghost kitchens." He acquired a company called CloudKitchens, a startup that rents

---

5   How Does Uber Make Money? www.investopedia.com/news/how-does-uber-make-money.

commercial space to delivery-only restaurants. Instead of operating and maintaining a full dine-in restaurant, CloudKitchens offers chefs a place to prepare food for their customers. By eliminating the dine-in portion of the business, restaurateurs can keep startup costs and overhead low by simply renting the kitchen space, then outsourcing food deliveries to gig workers through Uber Eats, DoorDash, and GrubHub, among other similar services.

In light of COVID-19 that spread during 2020, I expect this business idea to flourish. Sure, restaurants that deliver are convenient, but more importantly, restaurant delivery has the potential to evolve into more of a lifestyle than simply a factor of convenience.

Some of these companies not only had growth in mind but also deployed a take-no-prisoners mindset. Uber, for example, started providing their transportation services in cities before the legislation said they could do so. Uber did it anyway, and once enough of the city's citizens signed up and started using their services, the local government couldn't do much to reverse things, so they updated their legislation to allow the new business.

Bird, an electric-scooter-sharing platform based in Santa Monica, California, adopted this strategy as well. Before launching in their hometown, Bird's CEO sent a LinkedIn message to Santa Monica Mayor Ted Winterer asking for a meeting regarding the scooters. The mayor quickly replied, saying he'd meet with him, but when that meeting didn't happen, Bird put out its scooters anyway.[6] They were a hit. People started using them, and the city later changed its legislation to make them legal.

Although ethically questionable, this approach is great for the rapid advancement of innovation. If Bird had waited for permission to drop off their scooters, they likely would have struggled to find the success they did.

GAME CHANGERS: TECHNOLOGY

In addition to a growth mindset, the gig economy also grew thanks to technology. Modern technology is more powerful and efficient than ever before. Without it, none of these gig

---

6   https://www.cnet.com/news/
     the-electric-scooter-invasion-is-underway-bird-ceo-travis-vanderzanden-leads-the-charge/.

companies would have taken off twenty-five years ago, and certainly not this fast.

AMAZON WEB SERVICES (AWS)

Do you remember the red DVD envelopes Netflix used to mail out? Believe it or not, that was a cutting-edge choice at the time, but it was also the only thing that Reed Hastings, the CEO, had to work with. He had even more efficiency in mind, but the technology required for streaming video just wasn't there yet. It would be, soon, and when streaming became viable, Hastings was ready to leverage that technology to scale Netflix's streaming business.

One of the reasons Netflix was able to become the Netflix we know today is because of cloud computing services like Amazon Web Services (AWS). AWS is a secure cloud services platform, offering computing power, database storage, content delivery, and other functionality to help businesses scale and grow. Whether it's technology giants, television networks, banks, food manufacturers, or governments, many different organizations are using AWS to develop, deploy, and host applications—and Netflix happens to be one of their biggest clients.

AWS BIGGEST SPENDERS

The top ten AWS users based on EC2 monthly spend are:[7]

1. Netflix: $19 million.
2. Twitch: $15 million.
3. LinkedIn: $13 million.
4. Facebook: $11 million.
5. Turner Broadcasting: $10 million.
6. BBC: $9 million.
7. Baidu: $9 million.
8. ESPN: $8 million.
9. Adobe: $8 million.
10. Twitter: $7 million.

AWS is an opportunity for mastering gig work. Organizations need individuals with cloud skills to help transform their business. Cloud computing will lead to even more gig platforms and industry disruption as it gets more and more efficient as time goes on. If you master AWS now, when more platforms are built on it, you'll have more work since those companies will need people to do AWS for them.

The best part? AWS offers training and certification, both online and in person. Visit aws.amazon.com/training to learn more.

---

7   Who's Using Amazon Web Services? [2020 Update] https://www.contino.io/insights/
    whos-using-aws.

We've seen the transformational power of new technology before, during the Industrial Revolution, when European and American economies transitioned from hand production to machine production. New technologies, such as the automated assembly line, allowed them to be incredibly efficient.

Visionary businessmen throughout history, like Henry Ford, Thomas Edison, Mark Zuckerberg, and Jeff Bezos, wanted to bring their inventions and products to the masses, but they did so in a way that destroyed the competition. They'd drop their prices and take a loss on transactions, so their competitors were forced to do the same in order to stay relevant and compete. They were aggressive and would employ economic tactics so they could continue holding the most market share, the most money, and the most power. If a company managed to succeed through these tactics employed by their competitors, they would often get bought out and consumed by the bigger company. Facebook buying Instagram comes to mind as a modern example.

Companies in the gig economy are doing the same. Uber wants to be the biggest transportation company, even though there are a handful of others out there, with Lyft being their biggest competitor. Airbnb wants to be the biggest home-sharing company, with VRBO being their biggest competitor. Bird wants to be the main scooter company, even though there are dozens of other similar companies.

Lime, for example, is a huge one that was recently acquired by Uber.

As technology continues to change rapidly, companies adapt and implement changes as well. When Uber first launched, they used text messaging to inform customers of their driver's arrival. Now they use geolocation and communicate through the app that is installed directly on a user's smartphone. Riders can see a picture of the car that will pick them up, along with a photo of the driver. As technology changes, the ways these companies operate will also continue to change.

COMPETITION IS FIERCE

Like the rise of the factory production system, the rise of easy-to-use tech is a double-edged sword. The good news: technology enables strategic, analytical people to think through their business plans and reach greater levels of success much faster. The bad news: they can also fail much faster because accessible technology can make it look easy to start and run a business when it's not. Twenty years ago, for example, you had to learn HTML to create a website for your business. Before you committed to that, you would probably want to do a good amount of planning. Today, anyone can make a pretty good-looking site in thirty minutes (we show you how to build one, from start to finish, on bloggingtips.com). Even so, that doesn't mean they're ready to compete in the marketplace.

That's because the competition today is fierce. Back in 2008, just about anyone with a solid idea could jump into the gig economy and experience some success. Today, I tell aspiring entrepreneurs they'd better have a very, very, *very* good plan in place if they want to compete with the handful of tech companies that run this world. These companies not only have the best technology, they have the money to make the most of it; many have acquired incredible venture capital support. If you don't, you either have to find a way to out-scale the competition, differentiate yourself sufficiently, or build something one of the big guys will eventually acquire. If you're starting a delivery service, for instance, you need to analyze what Uber Eats and others are doing. Juno,[8] a ride-sharing company based in New York, was shut down in late 2019 because the company failed to carve out market share on the same turf as Lyft and Uber. You have to be deliberate and understand your role in this niche *before* you start your company.

Take HomeJoy as another example; one of the first platform companies to disrupt the $400 billion home cleaning market. Launched in 2010 in San Francisco, HomeJoy used a digital platform to connect homeowners with home cleaners that performed the service at a low rate. HomeJoy had the potential to become Silicon Valley's next unicorn, but unfortunately, mistakes were made, and by 2015, the com-

---

8   www.calcalistech.com/ctech/articles/0,7340,L-3773972,00.html.

pany was shut down, turning into a cautionary tale for other platform businesses.

A cleaning company typically charges at least $85 for a two-and-a-half-hour house cleaning, but HomeJoy offered new customers a promotional price of $19 per cleaning. While many platform companies subsidize products and services to fuel growth, HomeJoy's promotional price led to substantial losses, since 75 percent of their bookings came from discounts as opposed to referrals or organic traffic. Their promotional price also attracted the wrong customer: homeowners who were not willing to pay the full price of $25-35 an hour after their first heavily subsidized cleaning. HomeJoy's high customer acquisition costs were compounded by their retention problems, and the company started to run out of money.

To make matters worse, another nail in the coffin that led to HomeJoy's failure was an abundance of worker classification lawsuits, which claimed that HomeJoy treated cleaners as independent workers, thus depriving them of reimbursements and overtime wages. This argument is essentially the basis behind a recent bill from California legislators, called AB-5, which we'll discuss later in this book.

THE SECOND WAVE

All of this competition among gig companies creates an

opportunity for people looking for independent work. As companies continue to compete, they continue to innovate, creating an astounding range of prospects for workers even as the traditional job market shrinks.

People are catching on:[9]

- Already, 368,000 Americans search for work-at-home jobs on Google each month.
- From 2014 to 2018, the freelance workforce grew from 53 million to 56.7 million.
- Almost half of the millennials currently freelance.
- By 2021, gig workers will outnumber traditional employees.
- By 2027, the majority of the United States workforce is predicted to be involved in the gig economy.

The gig economy isn't just coming; it's already here. In this second wave of gig economy growth, independent work will become more than just an option; it will become the norm. This is especially true in light of the COVID-19 pandemic; more on this later. The overall trend is people are more interested in the gig economy, and there are more opportunities now than there were even five years ago thanks to technology and app-based platforms. It's time for you to accept the revolution and jump on board.

---

9   Freelancing in America, 2017 report.

In the next chapter, we'll talk about the current state of the gig economy.

CHAPTER TWO

———

THE CURRENT STATE OF THE GIG ECONOMY

Someone like Sam, the full-time developer we met in the introduction, might not know how fast the gig economy is expanding and what new opportunities exist. In this chapter, we'll define some common gig terminology, the type of people attracted to gig work, and why they joined the gig economy.

We'll also discuss the impact COVID-19 had and continues to have. The number of people working in the gig economy year over year continues to grow—and it will grow even faster thanks to the effects of COVID-19.

GIG TERMINOLOGY

Before we dive into the current state of the gig economy, let's explore some of the different terminology used.

All gig economy work is contractor based. This is also synonymous with receiving no benefits on behalf of a company. When it comes to tax time, you'll be filing your tax return using a 1099 as opposed to a W-2. As a contractor, you don't actually work for the company as an employee. Instead, it's more like a transaction. The company is looking for a specific project to be done, and they hire you to do that one project. It could take an hour, or it could take a year.

In the gig economy, there are a ton of platform-based gigs, like what we see with Airbnb, Uber, Task Rabbit, etc. These are companies that contract with gig workers in order for their business to run. The company manages everything—including how and when you're paid—and they also match supply and demand. If you work for an app-based platform, you work within the constraints of the company. You do the job they need you to do, how they want you to do it, but for the most part, you choose when to do it. With Uber, for example, you log into the driver app, activate driver mode, and pick up riders when it works for your schedule. Once you're done, you can simply log off and be done until you decide to drive again.

And then there's freelancing. Freelancing is much more

independent. You are your own business, essentially, which means you are in charge of everything: marketing yourself, getting clients, negotiating contracts, completing the work, sending out invoices, and so on. In regard to strategy and planning, freelancing is very hands-on, whereas platform gigs are very hands-off.

Although both can be considered being self-employed, I draw a more distinct line: self-employment, to me, is when you run your own business. Say you're a designer who designs print collateral for various clients. That's freelance work. But if you were to start a design agency that then contracts with other services—say, bookkeeping, for example— then I'd consider that self-employment.

You can be one, both, or all three. As an Uber driver, I was an app-based gig worker. When I designed websites for people, I was a freelancer, and now—since I run my own business that contracts with gig workers— I'm also self-employed. While companies technically pay me as a 1099 contractor, I'm no longer just doing contract work. I'm building something for myself that's sustainable over the long term.

Gigs are mostly one-off projects. If you're doing lighting for a band, for example, that's a gig—even if you do that over the span of a few nights. If you're the lighting director for a band and you tour with them, on the other hand, that's a contract.

So which gig avenue is right for you? That depends heavily on your talents, goals, expectations, and ambitions. There's something out there for everyone, so let's see what type of people are joining the gig economy.

WHO IS GETTING IN ON THE GIG?

In the United States today, more than one in three workers have done some sort of gig work. Among people in traditional jobs like Sam's, one in six would like to switch to the gig economy full time. That's 79 to 129 million people who say they want to leave their traditional jobs.[10]

Many of these people are like Sam or like Lily, a freelance graphic designer I work with. She's amazingly talented; she has a knack for integrating a brand into every aspect of a business. She is also a very caring person and needs to spend a lot of time with her ailing mother, so a traditional work schedule would not work for her. Freelancing for my company, among her many other clients, is much more ideal. When she works on projects with my team, I really don't care when or where she does the work, only that she does it by the time we need it done. She has helped us out in a pinch more than once, and she's free to travel to another state or country while still practicing her craft, earning an income.

---

10   2017 State of Telecommuting in the U.S. Employee Workforce and Brett's own data.

AGES AND STAGES

Every gig worker's story is different, but I have noticed some trends among different age groups as they enter the gig economy: recent college graduates (roughly between the ages of twenty to twenty-five), mid-career professionals (roughly between the ages of twenty-five to fifty), and those near or in retirement (ages fifty and beyond).

Recent College Graduates

Newly minted graduates are the most likely to jump in feet first, without requiring much guidance. They tend to be comfortable learning everything on the fly because that's the culture they've grown up in. After all, many of their friends are doing it, too, so it seems normal.

They also don't yet have established careers, families, or other obligations that may make entering the gig economy difficult. Recent grads aren't ingrained with the thought of working for one company for thirty years, either. It's normal to jump from one job to the next. It's sort of like dating but for careers. They don't mind bouncing around to see what they like. The technology also helps. There are many more options today than there were even just a few years ago. They haven't been working for long, slogging away at one company for ten years like our friend, Sam. They haven't spent much time trying to advance in a company, only to be left frustrated.

A lot of younger people these days crave freedom and flexibility because they want to travel. They long for a lifestyle that allows them to get on a plane and see the world. Thanks in part to social media influencers who post about their travel adventures, recent college graduates who might not know exactly what they want to do in life are attracted to this travel lifestyle—which then leads them to look for jobs or a career that would offer that to them. Because they're often unmarried with nothing like a mortgage to tie them down to a particular location, these young people don't mind working in a different city every few months. They'd also rather spend their money on experiences, not material possessions, unlike those in previous generations. Young people are also more open-minded to trying new things, even if it doesn't directly line up with their chosen field. Gig life, thus, is a perfect fit.

Young adults gravitate toward gigs that use their creative and technical skills. As those skills evolve and get noticed, they move up to bigger opportunities. Many are like my father was years ago; he got into the event planning industry when he agreed to make a flyer for someone, although he had never designed a flyer before. At the time, he had little idea what he was doing, but he saw the chance to get noticed and took it. He ended up teaching himself and did such a good job, he was eventually asked to plan entire events himself. Despite his initial lack of experience, he jumped in with both feet and grew a simple opportunity into a successful business for himself.

The same thing happened to me. I started publishing information for rideshare drivers, only to have it evolve into an entire career of its own. You never know where the gig economy is going to take you.

Young gig workers might be graphic designers or video editors doing something similar—building their portfolios through gig work and seeing where it leads. Some strike out on their own right away, but more often, they work for an agency full time and moonlight on the side at first. Because they're usually single and childless, they can put a lot of time and energy into their gig work.

As an employer, I love working with these people because they bring a high level of energy and expertise to the work. And since I run websites about gig work using a team that is made up of only 1099 contractors, I can scale up and down as rapidly as needed, allowing my business to have the flexibility that many others do not.

Mid-Career Professionals

You might think that people who have been in the workforce for a while would also seek creative work because their accumulated experience and skills seem so transferrable to independent work. Surely a career accountant would launch an accounting business of their own, right? Wrong. Surprisingly, mid-career professionals often take a sharp turn looking for something entirely new when they leave their old jobs. Many enter the gig economy through easily available, app-based gigs instead. They drive for Uber, walk dogs, or tutor kids. Some are undoubtedly burned out on their careers and looking for a low-stress alternative. Others may feel intimidated by the thought of learning a new skill. Often, they're simply strapped for time because they're still in the thick of raising children and/or caring for aging parents. On the other hand, some have too much time on their hands; their kids went off to college, and they're just looking for a lucrative way to fill empty hours.

Some people who make the jump to gig work at mid-life unnecessarily hold themselves back from interesting options because they worry that their skills are outdated or that they'll have to learn complicated technologies in order to succeed. That may be true to some extent, but if they investigate, they'll discover that the technology is not difficult to master; it's much easier to use now than it was just ten—or even five—years ago. If you're accomplished in your field and think that might translate over to gig work, it's worth finding out what you need to do to come up to speed.

Retirement Age

As retirement age approaches, many people come to realize their nest isn't feathered quite as well as they'd like it to be. Or at all. In the United States, 51 percent of people over age fifty-five aren't where they should be when it comes to retirement savings. When they face the financial facts, near-retirees often look to build their savings with exactly what the gig economy has to offer—simple jobs with a low barrier of entry.

People near retirement age are increasingly taking nontraditional jobs. According to the federal Bureau of Labor Statistics, an estimated 11.4 percent of people between the ages of fifty and sixty-two have nontraditional jobs. The Government Accounting Office says this figure is even higher—31.2 percent. For those over sixty-two, as much as 9 percent of people were in "on-call, temp, contract, or gig jobs" in 2015, according to economists at the New School's Retirement Equity Lab.[11]

At all ages, people's priorities are shifting from remaining at one job for life, for security, to getting the most they can out of their entire life. People see freelance work as a chance to liberate themselves from conventional jobs so they can pursue the lifestyle they *really* want.

WHY ARE PEOPLE SEEKING GIG WORK?

Like our designer, many gig workers are looking for work-life balance. Most freelancers cite freedom and flexibility as top reasons for making the jump.

---

11   https://www.nytimes.com/2019/10/25/health/seniors-nontraditional-jobs.
html?searchResultPosition=2.

They are also in it for the money:[12]

- Forty percent of independent workers are in it to make extra money; it's a secondary source of income.
- Fourteen percent wouldn't say gig work was their first choice, but they need the money and gig jobs are readily available. Gigs provide their primary source of income.
- Sixteen percent struggle to pay the bills each month, so they pick up independent work to make ends meet.
- Forty-two percent of people freelance for the simple reason that they're unable to work a full-time job.
- Half of people have no retirement savings and look to gig work to fund their retirement years.
- Forty-two percent freelance because they are unable to find full-time jobs.
- Other reasons people seek gig work:
  - Childcare costs are rising.
  - Personal health issues.
  - Caregiving for parents, spouses, or kids.

And although there are no current studies with data from 2020, I'm betting that the coronavirus pandemic has created strong incentives for people to join the gig economy.

---

12 James Manyika, Susan Lund, Jacques Bughin, Kelsey Robinson, Jan Mischke, and Deepa Mahajan, McKinsey Global Institute, "Independent Work: Choice, Necessity, and the Gig Economy," October 2016.

IMPACT FROM COVID-19

As the coronavirus pandemic swept the world in 2020, it disrupted everything in its wake. While millions of people lost their jobs, millions more started to work from home for the first time. COVID-19 could very well be the catalyst for more companies to adopt remote work in the long run—and it won't just be for temporary work, either.

Before COVID-19, many companies were somewhat resistant to freelance, contractor, or gig work. But then COVID-19 came around and forced them into a trial by fire. Governments ordered businesses to shut down to limit in-person contact and those who had the ability to work remotely did. We also saw an increased popularity of video conferencing tools like Zoom and UberConference. I believe a whole slew of new services will pop up, too. People who are working from home for the first time will grow frustrated with something and figure out a way to solve it.

Despite the tragic deaths from COVID-19, when it comes to the gig economy, the pandemic will have catapulted gig work further and faster than anyone could have ever planned.

There will be a huge shift in how people view remote work, regardless of industry. Naturally, there will be industries that will be less affected than others, but for the industries where face-to-face interaction isn't a necessity, we will see a lot of changes to make things more efficient and cost-effective. The definition of networking will change. Instead of going to conferences or networking events to boost your businesses, it will be more acceptable to conduct virtual meetings. People might still prefer face-to-face interaction, but whereas video conferencing was barely an option before, it will be far more prevalent in the future. Financial advisors, lawyers, and salespeople will increasingly lean on video conferencing without judgment. For those roles, business might grow as these professions could potentially increase their reach from a geographical location to a virtual one, which is seemingly limitless.

For example, my friend Brady, one of the best financial planners I know, was in the right place at the right time. Before COVID-19, he had talked with me at length about taking his financial planning practice virtual so that he would have the freedom and flexibility to travel the world while still running his business. Since he is a 1099 contractor for the firm he works with, he is only responsible for his own clients and can manage them however he thinks best. Now that his clients are accustomed to virtual meetings because of COVID-19, it looks like his dream of managing clients virtually is one step closer to becoming a reality.

There are several money-saving opportunities for businesses moving forward. By increasing virtual client interaction, they don't have to send their salespeople out all the time. Will companies opt to send their people across the country and pay for all the expenses when a virtual meeting can be done at very little cost? In corporations, perhaps they'll be more interested in hiring the right person, regardless of their location, instead of hiring the best candidate that is willing to relocate to physically work in their office. I hope they question the need for in-person meetings and choose to use virtual conferencing for people who can still be productive yet need to take care of a child or an aging parent at home. Think about all the money companies can save on rent if they let go of an office and commit to a remote-only staff. Companies can save hundreds or thousands of dollars a year, if not more.

For whatever reason, remote work tends to have a bad rap. A lot of bosses think workers can't be productive at home. There's definitely a learning curve, and people need to spend the time to figure out what works best for them, but COVID-19 forced the masses to work from home and shattered this misconception.

When I first dove into gig work full time, it was incredibly hard for me to get into the habit of being productive. I couldn't focus on my work, and everything became a distraction to me. And when I say everything, I mean *everything*: eating, sleeping, spontaneously working out, playing with my dog, doing laundry, cleaning my house, and so on.

I kid you not. I would find myself diving down rabbit holes of immense unproductivity, anything but sitting at my computer to put in the hours. I would mow my lawn, for example, and upon completing that task, I would find something else to do to my yard, like re-mulching my landscaping. After that was done, I'd take my dog for a walk. I'd inevitably realize that he could use a bath, so then I'd give him one.

I chased these rabbit holes for about a month before realizing something needed to change. My solution? Going to coffee shops. By packing up my things and intentionally going to a coffee shop, I physically removed myself from the distractions. I found a small mom-and-pop coffee shop in my city and became a regular to the point where the baristas had my drink ready upon my arrival. I'd take my black coffee in the largest size they offered and find an empty table to work. I'd put my Bose noise-canceling headphones over my ears, press play on a bass-heavy, electronic playlist, and buckle in for a day of productivity. And it worked. Without the distractions of home life, I consistently completed my work. Since then, I've upgraded my office situation and now work in an office space I rent. More on that later.

In light of the pandemic, working in coffee shops or an office space might not be an option. If you are unable to work from a public space, you'll have to figure out how to set up your home to reduce distractions. I know someone who worked in his car from his driveway since his wife and two kids were also home and were too distracting for him. Another colleague created an office space in the spare bedroom of her house. She would tell her family she's "going to work" and then lock herself in the bedroom until she was done working. Another friend constructed a tiny shed in the back of his house and made that his workspace.

Another outcome we'll see from COVID-19 is the increase in fractional work. Instead of hiring a full-time accountant as an employee, a company will just hire someone when they need them. Do you need someone on staff to do your accounting for $60,000 a year when you can hire someone just as good as a contractor for $2,000 a month to keep your books and run reports? I think not.

This is not only true of legal services but also the entire C suite. Finance, for example, is being outsourced to fractional companies like CFO Systems, a company that my uncle works at. Instead of hiring a full-time finance director internally, you can hire one of the company's fractional CFO's—industry experts with decades of experience in the finance field—to spearhead those efforts.

We will see a lot of changes in the future where businesses become more efficient by eliminating a lot of the inefficiencies that they are accustomed to paying for.

COVID-19 also forced people into using technology. For anyone who previously avoided learning how to use Face-Time or any number of video conferencing apps, COVID-19 forced them to learn to use it. Otherwise, they wouldn't see their children or their grandchildren. CEOs who belong in the older generation were forced to utilize technology to manage their employees and do their best to move through the business challenges COVID-19 presented.

And if I'm being honest, it's about time. The benefits of the gig economy are here to stay. Even though the gig economy was heading in this direction, COVID-19 enhanced and expedited the process. The pandemic was the catalyst for the widespread adoption of remote work. That's where the world is now going. The time of resistance is over.

Once people start working independently, they're likely to stick with it. Of those who have taken the leap to freelance, a majority report that no amount of money would get them to take a traditional job again,[13] whether they're young or old because working independently is much better for their personalities and lifestyle. Traditional workers often describe their workday with words like routine, boredom, bureaucracy, and stressful, while independent workers use words like free, independent, and creative.[14]

---

13 Freelancing in America 2017.

14 Freelancing in America 2017.

I can surely relate. So much of my traditional work just didn't make much sense when I sat down and thought about it. Yet, it was frustrating and largely out of my control. I despise small talk, so the lengthy water cooler conversations about nothing related to work were always difficult for me to have. They seemed like an inefficient waste of time. And then there were the meetings I just couldn't find the motivation to be involved with. In my corporate days, for instance, I remember getting stuck in a four-hour meeting debating the definitions of a handful of safety training words that we never once used again after that meeting. In another, I listened to a company-wide hurricane briefing from a Fortune 500 company—and we were in the middle of landlocked Nebraska.

If I had an idea for a side hustle or a change to my Ridester website, I would have to wait until I got home to do those things. My full-time job always seemed to be getting in the way of my ideas, vision, and ambition. After all, the companies I worked for provided me a paycheck and rightfully expected my full attention during work hours.

While I am very appreciative of my experiences, I don't miss my corporate days at all.

Today, as I look out my window and see the office complex across the road, I wonder what they could possibly be doing in there. When I talk to the people who do work there, they ask the same question: What *are* we doing in here? Will we still be doing it ten or twenty years from now? More than half of U.S. workers think they might not be; they know their employment prospects are changing. If traditional jobs disappear, and they don't get into independent work, they will be left behind. At the same time, independent work has also become a more acceptable—even respected—choice.

That said, the gig lifestyle varies wildly. It can enable you to work nontraditional hours and save big chunks of time for the things you really want to do, whether that means taking scuba diving lessons or spending more time with the grandkids. It can help fund your family vacation. It can make retirement more comfortable. The list goes on.

It's not all bliss and glory, however. The gig lifestyle has developed some myths that I will break down in the next chapter, followed by some snippets of what life really looks like for a handful of gig workers.

CHAPTER THREE

MYTHS AND REALITIES OF THE GIG ECONOMY

If you're considering gig work, don't believe everything you hear. Some of it is pure myth. In this chapter, I'll dispel some of the most common myths around gig work, and then I'll share some brief highlights of what gig work *actually* looks like.

MYTH #1: GIG WORK IS EASY, FLEXIBLE, AND FUN!

I hear this one all the time from people considering independent work, and I can see why. From the outside, the gig life can look pretty sweet—you can sleep until noon every day, only work when you want to, and do what you love, right?

That's what my friend, who we'll call John, thought when he saw me driving for Uber and setting up Ridester. It looked easy. I drove only a few hours a day, and I was making what I considered to be pretty good money. What he didn't see was that I stayed up all night for two years straight to work on my business. He also didn't know about all the nights that I stayed at home to work instead of hanging out with my friends. He didn't know I was thinking, "Oh, crap, there's nobody here to hold my hand anymore—it's all up to me. If this doesn't work out, I will have wasted countless hours, many sleepless nights would be in vain, and the sacrifices I made to work on the business will be of no use to me at all."

He also didn't see the constant perseverance that I had when I was up against people that didn't believe in me. I distinctly recall multiple conversations with my professors and friends that were constantly telling me that nobody would use Ridester and that I should just give up on the idea and worry about a full-time corporate job instead of building what was, in my ex-girlfriend's words, a "stupid little website." Moments like those were trying, but amid the uncertainty and lack of support, I pushed through and kept grinding.

As far as he could see, there was no downside, so John quit his job and dove into his new life as a freelancer building websites that would cash flow his way to a life of passive income and freedom. That was an exciting thought, but it takes quite a few years for websites to get up and running, so in the meantime, he also had to take on contract jobs doing website design and SEO work for small businesses, which kept him too busy to promote his blogging business. He was so overwhelmed with work he couldn't keep up and eventually went back to a full-time job.

Although working in the gig economy can be flexible and fun, it's not without its drawbacks, which we will explore in future chapters. And it's anything but easy—after all, you're still working. Learning to enjoy the freedom and flexibility that freelancing offers comes with a steep learning curve. When you're working for yourself, being disciplined is vital to your success. When I first dived headfirst into gig work after leaving my dad's company, I didn't have the discipline I now have. In fact, it took about a year to really find a routine that focused on the work that needed to be done to unlock the freedom and flexibility I craved. You still have to put in the work, and part of that is having the discipline to schedule yourself appropriately.

Reality: Succeeding in the gig economy is a lot of work. It requires an immense amount of discipline and an entrepreneurial mindset.

MYTH #2: GIG WORK WILL MAKE ME RICH, FAST!

We've all heard the stories of people who got into the gig

economy early and made a bunch of money right away. It's tempting to think that will happen to you, too, but it's unlikely, largely because your earnings are usually limited by how many hours you can work in a day, week, month, or year.

If you get in with a well-funded new company in its earliest phases in the gig economy (we'll talk about the gig cycle in Chapter Five), they're oftentimes willing to pay higher rates and bonuses to get themselves launched. Think back to Uber's savage affiliate program that paid $1,000 to each new driver. If you time it right, the potential to make a lot of money quickly is there, but huge payouts are not that common. More importantly, those types of payouts or bonuses are not usually sustainable. In an effort to save money and work towards profitability, a well-funded gig company will oftentimes drop any guerrilla marketing programs as soon as they meet their market share goal.

Instead, expect to struggle to make money at first. I don't know how many times I've heard people say, "I've been driving Uber for two months, and I'm still broke," or "I'm renting out a house on Airbnb, and it feels like I'm just tossing money at it." When I hear these sorts of comments, that usually means they haven't done enough planning. Gig work is still work, and you have to be strategic and thoughtful about how you do that work. That being said, if you're losing money, it could mean it's time to throw in the towel on that particular gig. You should *never* be paying to work.

You can earn a decent income working in the gig economy by planning well and working hard. It is also possible to become wealthy in the gig economy but to do that, you'll have to level up. If you want to be a millionaire, you're going to need to develop a bigger business and maybe even become a gig employer yourself.

Reality: Gig work *might* make you rich but not right away, and certainly not without a lot of work.

MYTH #3: THE COMPANY WILL TAKE CARE OF ME

Most first-time gig workers are reluctant to take too big a risk by signing on with a new start-up they haven't heard of before. They prefer to go with the known entities: companies they are familiar with, such as Uber, Airbnb, or Lyft. That choice feels safe and stable, and people assume these well-known employers must treat their workers well. Unfortunately, these assumptions are not necessarily always true.

These big-name companies may give the impression that they're stable, but they're usually not. Their *modus operandi* is to "move fast and break things," as Mark Zuckerberg famously said, which means everything is subject to change at any moment. The job you sign up for this week may not be there next week; the company may not be either. That's not a problem for you in the long run because you have plenty of other options, but it can come as a shock if you were counting on them to be "too big to fail."

This is also why you should diversify and have more than one stream of income. There's high volatility when it comes to working for app-based companies. One day they're thriving, but they can disappear in an instant. Companies that provide a good amount of income for gig economy workers can dissolve overnight. A great example of this is Cargo, which shuttered its innovative Cargo box. The Cargo box was somewhat like a vending machine for rideshare drivers. Cargo provided an inventory of snacks and other miscellaneous items to drivers, who would then pass them out or sell them to their passengers during rides. Cargo would pay drivers for every free and paid item that was distributed to a passenger. Cargo made deals with companies to distribute free snacks to passengers as a way to build brand awareness for the snack company. As a result, drivers could make an extra $150-$500 a month by partnering with Cargo, in addition to the higher tips passengers often gave after receiving an unexpected snack for free.

Unfortunately, the company couldn't fully perfect that business model, and they were forced to shut that product down and take their company in a different direction. If you were an Uber driver who participated with Cargo and you earned an extra $500 per month, you lost that monthly $500 you became accustomed to earning in the blink of an eye. That's a car payment, rent, or groceries for the month—gone. Needless to say, there's a bit of volatility and risk involved when you work for app-based platforms.

The relationship between companies in the gig economy and their workers is very different from that of traditional employers with dedicated human resource departments. Some new gig workers also feel like the more established companies will provide some protection for them, but that's not usually true, either. This is evident, as a recent Ridester study[15] found that more than 46 percent of Uber drivers quit after one year or less. Of drivers surveyed, drivers gave Uber's corporate leadership less than three stars on a scale from one to five, and support operations barely over three stars.

I know a dog walker who has walked hundreds of dogs for Rover. One day, one of the dogs bit him, and he expected Rover to come to his aid, legally and financially. They did not, and my friend was furious. The reality is that dog walkers get bitten; it's a risk he knew he was taking and not the hiring company's fault or responsibility.

Reality: When you're an independent contractor, anything can happen, no matter who you work for. Don't let a big name lull you into a false sense of security.

---

15   https://www.ridester.com/2020-survey/.

MYTH #4: THERE'S NO PLACE FOR ME IN THE GIG ECONOMY

People think gig work is just for tech geeks, young people, or hustlers. Maybe that was once true, but new gigs emerge all the time. Remember to think outside the box!

For example, many established brands have given rise to specialty services, whether as offshoots of the original business or as competition in niche markets. Just consider the delivery services category. Do an online search, and you'll see DoorDash for general delivery, GrubHub and Caviar for food delivery, Drizly for liquor delivery, and GoPuff for snack delivery, just to name a few. By the time you finish reading this book, there will likely be another new delivery app available on your phone.

Everybody is trying to keep up with the original disruptors. Uber was once the only rideshare game in town, but now Lyft challenges that position. Next thing we knew, Via popped up. Now, there is even HopSkipDrive aimed specifically at providing kids with safe rides.

If you think there's nothing out there for you, think again because the variety of opportunities for independent workers is stunning. You can rent out your home, parking spot, tools, or even your boat. You can make meals in someone else's house, take care of their grandmother, or do their taxes.

If you're already driving for Uber, you can easily opt into driving for their other offerings, like Uber Eats and their package delivery service. Since you've already been vetted and approved by the ridesharing company, the approval process for additional Uber services is quick and painless. Once approved, from the same Uber app, you can toggle back and forth between Uber and Uber Eats, and plan your day where you're giving rides in the morning, delivering food over lunch hours, and then back to giving rides in the evening. In theory, one can sign up to drive for Uber and stay busy all the time because there is what seems like a never-ending supply of delivery options available.

In the past ten years, more and more professional jobs have moved into the gig economy as well. Designers, copywriters, accountants, and even lawyers can grab gigs on platforms like Upwork, Fiverr, or Freelancer.com. I've personally hired many of these types of professionals through freelance platforms and have been pleasantly surprised with the work they've provided.

Reality: With such a wide array of gigs available, and new ones on the horizon, there is likely an appropriate place in the gig economy for you.

WHAT GIG WORK *REALLY* LOOKS LIKE

Here's a sampling of what the gig lifestyle can look like:

Imagine you're a twenty-two-year-old standing around at a party when your phone rings. It's an Uber request—you've got to go. You might be back in an hour, or you might be out the whole night giving rides. If that sounds chaotic, it is, but it worked perfectly for a friend of mine. He loves driving for Uber, giving rides, and meeting new people. He has great stories about the NBA player he ferried through town and the high-profile keynote speaker he drove from Omaha to Lincoln, Nebraska. Even better, he could arrange his schedule around his life. He worked in sprints—sometimes working for two weeks at a time without a real break—to make money to fund an upcoming vacation. He loved it and still does because it lets him do the things he wants to do.

Of course, ridesharing is not limited to college-aged students. Plenty of retired folks choose to drive for Uber or Lyft as a way to supplement income, bolster their retirement, or engage with people for a little fun.

MY FAVORITE RIDESHARE COMPANIES

1. Uber
2. Lyft
3. Curb
4. Gett
5. Via

RENT OUT YOUR CAR, DRIVEWAY, HOME, STUFF, ETC.

The term "rentals" covers a wide variety of options. Do you live in a city where parking is a problem? You can rent out your driveway with sites like Spothero.com. There are plenty of websites that make renting parking spaces easier. Maybe you're traveling, and you're not going to use your work spot; well, you can rent that out while you're gone.

Then, of course, we have home rentals, with websites like Airbnb and VRBO.

You can even rent your car out with sites like Turo and HyreCar. I know a guy who rents out his Tesla and makes a pretty penny on the side (although I'm not sure I would trust strangers to drive a Tesla, but hey, to each their own).

Just as ridesharing allows drivers to make money with their car when they aren't using it for personal reasons, you can make money renting out other things you own, too, like tools, a boat, cameras, a motorcycle, and so on.

You can even rent a friend. At RentAFriend.com, "friends" from around the world are available for hire. People who travel to a new city can hire a local to show them around town. If you want to go see a movie but don't have anyone to go with, you can rent a friend to join you.

MY RECOMMENDED RENTAL PLATFORMS

Rent your home: Airbnb or Homeaway

Rent your RV: Outdoorsy

Rent your car: Turo or HyreCar

Rent your airplane: OpenAirplane

Rent your parking space: JustPark or SpotHero

Rent your boat: GetMyBoat

FOOD/PACKAGE DELIVERY

There are a variety of food delivery services out there, like Uber Eats, Postmates, GrubHub, and DoorDash. As the driver, your app will tell you where to pick up food and where to deliver it to—that's pretty much it. It's very transactional and is considered low-skill work since there's little more to the gig other than keeping the food safe and getting it from Point A to Point B. Arguably, this gig is the easiest gig of them all.

On the customer side, the app offers a straightforward user experience. Users can see the restaurants that participate, their hours, and their menus. The app also handles payments. Once a user makes their selection, they check out and pay for it, and then the driver is notified to pick up and deliver.

When it comes to driving routes for food delivery, however, there's not much planning that you can do. You're at the whim of customers and where they order from. You can finish making a delivery, and then your next delivery could be twenty miles away, but you have to backtrack to the restaurant to pick up the food. It's hard to build in efficiencies. Although this is one of the easiest gigs, you probably won't make a ton of money after you factor in the cost of mileage, gas, and depreciation of your vehicle.

Package delivery is a bit different because it's more structured and predictable. Take working with Amazon Flex, for example. Drivers will go to a centralized Amazon Fulfillment center, pick up some of the packages scheduled to be delivered that day, and head out on their route. If they finish and would like to do a second route, they can return to the warehouse and pick up a slew of packages for another route. As long as they sign up for available delivery blocks, they'll be working set hours they sign up for ahead of time.

UNIQUE DELIVERY APPS

goPuff – Snack delivery

Drizly – Alcohol delivery

Amazon Flex – Package delivery

GROCERY SHOPPING/DELIVERY

When it comes to grocery shopping and delivery, like the app Instacart, for example, there are two positions: the shopper and the full-service shopper. Customers create their shopping list and then place an order using an app that manages the logistics of somebody else that does the shopping for them. As a gig worker, once a customer uploads their grocery list to the app, you'll receive a notification to go to the store to shop for this person. Once you've collected their milk, bread, orange juice, and chicken, you'll check out and pay for the groceries with a prepaid credit card provided to you by Instacart. At this point, the customer is notified that their order is ready, and they can either choose to pick it up from the store, or they can choose to have it delivered to their home or workplace. If you are an in-store shopper, you are responsible for just shopping in the store for multiple Instacart customers. If you are a full-service shopper, you are responsible for doing both the shopping and the delivery to the customer.

In markets of very high demand like San Francisco and New York, there's a ton of people signing up for these services. As such, the person shopping and the person delivering are most likely two different people. In smaller markets in rural areas, you're likely to see the same person doing both jobs.

Lots of major grocery store chains, like Ralph's, Kroger, and Walmart, have grocery shopping as an option for their own employees to do, but they typically contract the delivery portion with independent contractors.

COVID-19 has been the catalyst for the mass adoption of food and grocery delivery services. As lockdowns began nationwide, these services exploded in popularity. Instacart, for example, went on a hiring spree and hired hundreds of thousands of shoppers to fulfill the insane demand that they experienced.

These companies did a great job in pivoting their business models to ensure simplicity, safety, and effectiveness. If you order food from Uber Eats, for example, you are able to select a contactless delivery option within the app. The delivery driver will leave the food outside your door, take a picture of where he left it, and then upload that picture to the Uber Eats app, notifying you of the successful delivery.

Like we talked about earlier, if you see trends like this, you can jump on board the bandwagon and make money during the company's early stages while the going is good.

VIRTUAL/PERSONAL ASSISTANTS

Many people look at VAs as little more than executive assistants, but this role can be much more than repetitive administrative work. In its broadest form, a virtual assistant is anyone who offers services to other individuals or businesses from afar in exchange for an agreed-upon fee. Services include customer support, processing online orders and refunds, calendar management and travel arrangements, transcription, content research, and email management.

Many large companies like Apple, American Express, and Amazon, to name a few, contract their customer support to 1099 contractors. In past decades, these customer support representatives worked from huge call centers; however, now, with the advent of technology, many of these representatives work from home. The next time you're on a call with a customer support agent, pay particular attention to background noise. If you listen closely, you can oftentimes hear a dog barking in the background, which typically means the representative is working from home.

Personal assistants fall under the same umbrella, but their tasks are more personal. Services include shopping for groceries, picking kids up from school or daycare, taking the dog for a walk, putting away laundry, etc. It's similar to a nanny, without living on the premises. Personal assistants, not surprisingly, are very popular with more affluent neighborhoods.

SCOOTER CHARGERS

If you've been to a big city, you've likely seen scooters scattered around sidewalks and in front of businesses. There are a ton of scooter companies now, and they're always looking for independent contractors to help them corral their existing inventory, whether that means collecting them up from a far-off location or picking up and charging them overnight.

As one of these contractors, your responsibility would be to collect these scooters at night and either return them to a centralized warehouse for maintenance and repairs or take them home to charge them. The scooter company supplies you with the necessary charging apparatuses, and your job is to charge a certain number of scooters every night and return them to the streets the following morning. Scooter chargers get paid pretty well, too: many report making hundreds, if not thousands, of dollars every month. Gig workers with large scooter charging operations can even make six figures if they do enough volume.

The last time I was in Los Angeles eating dinner with a friend at a restaurant, there was quite a bit of commotion on the street outside the building. When I looked to see what was happening, I saw a man placing scooters from the street into a huge trailer where there must have been a minimum of one hundred scooters. He probably did that for a living and made some good money doing so.

RANDOM TASKS

Are you handy with a hammer? Are you talented with appliance repairs? If you're good at any number of tasks, you can find work on apps like TaskRabbit or TAKL. TaskRabbit is an on-demand freelance site that includes all sorts of jobs, from housekeeping to handyman work to helping someone move boxes.

Say you're really good at building IKEA furniture. You'd list furniture building as one of your skills in your profile, and the app would match you with people in your area that need that service. You would then go over to the client's house, help them build the furniture, and get paid through the app once you finished.

Side note: IKEA bought TaskRabbit in 2017 as part of an effort to increase different services meant to help customers after they purchase "assemble-yourself" furniture.

TEACHING ENGLISH

Maybe you have a degree in English, journalism, or communication, or you're really adept in the English language. If so, you should check out teaching English online. Although advanced credentials will help you stand out among the competition, most English teaching platforms don't require tutors to have degrees.

English as a second language is becoming a booming trend. There are now entire platforms dedicated to pairing English tutors with students looking to learn. As a result of that demand, wages for tutors are increasing, making now a great time to check out this gig.

SOME ONLINE ENGLISH TEACHING OPTIONS[16]

1. VIPKid pays $22 an hour.
2. Dadada pays $25 an hour.
3. Chegg Tutors pays $20 an hour.
4. Teachaway pays between $20 to $25 an hour.
5. QKids pays up to $20 an hour.

GRAPHIC DESIGN

If you know how to design ads, websites, or posters, joining a platform like Upwork or Fiverr is a great way to remove the friction that arises when sourcing clients and managing bids, contracts, and payments.

Fiverr started out as a weird niche part of the internet where you could get anything done for $5—and I mean *anything*. Sure, tasks like color-correcting photos, editing blog posts, or converting files to PDF were listed for $5, but there were some bizarre listings, too. For example, you could pay a stranger to record themselves singing happy birthday to send to a friend. Over time, however, Fiverr has become a

---

16 These amounts are as of this book's publishing in 2020 and are subject to change.

very robust marketplace for service transactions. As Fiverr grew, so did their prices, but you can still find plenty of tasks offered at $5.

As a designer, depending on the scope of the project, you can charge accordingly. Say you are browsing for work and see a request from someone looking to create a custom header image for an email campaign. You bid on the project with your price and then wait to see if your bid is accepted. Once accepted, you complete the task and get paid.

Fiverr isn't just for designers. You can find everything under the sun there. From highly technical gigs like software development and testing to fun gigs like impersonating celebrities and doing pranks, there's an opportunity for everyone to make money. Upwork is another option—still a gig marketplace but a more curated, higher quality version of Fiverr.

These marketplaces are successful because they act like the middle man between transactions. Instead of getting scammed by a client who refuses to pay you after you've completed the work, these marketplaces facilitate the contracts, the expectations, and the payments. These platforms go out of their way to ensure the smoothest, most frictionless experience for both buyer and seller.

CAREGIVING FOR PEOPLE AND ANIMALS

Do you have experience as an adult caregiver? Join one of the online care platforms like SitterCity.com or Care.com, and find local families looking for someone like you to help care for their loved ones. Create a profile that lists your skills, such as CPR and first aid training, household skills like cooking and cleaning, and whether you have specialty skills, like experience with Alzheimer's and dementia. Both SitterCity.com and Care.com look for nannies, childcare, elderly care, special needs care, and pet care providers.

Imagine you have a full-time job that includes a lot of traveling. You really want a dog, but with your work schedule and travel, you can't really commit to one. Well, how about renting one?

This sounds ridiculous, but I actually know someone who does this. She signed up on Rover.com, a pet sitting site, to source her dogs. Depending on her schedule, she gets paid while watching someone else's dog. She's not in it for the money, so she only works when it works for her. She just does it so she can have a dog when she wants a dog, without the responsibility of owning one herself.

CAREGIVING APPS

SitterCity

Care.com

UrbanSitter

DogVacay

Rover

Wag

Papa

DIGITAL MARKETER

Maybe you don't feel like you could be put in a box, which is how my friend Haris felt. He dropped out of college because he found it just wasn't for him. He worked at a car dealership detailing cars until he landed an internship with Vayner Media in New York, working for entrepreneur and best-selling author Gary Vaynerchuk. After that, he was hooked on digital marketing.

Over time, Haris has cultivated a list of clients, and he'll fly to wherever they are to work for them. He flew out to San Francisco to help a music artist push out a recently launched podcast and helped her market it on Facebook, Instagram, and other social media platforms.

This might sound glamorous, but he had to network his way to success—and it didn't happen overnight. He worked hard, and he sacrificed a lot to get to where he is today. Another advantage for him is that he takes the opportunity to learn from his clients. While he's being hired to work for them, he also learns from these successful people—something that the average nine-to-fiver simply doesn't have access to.

GETTING STARTED

A few of my favorite courses:

1. AuthorityHacker.com – Learn how to create powerful authority websites.
2. BackLinko.com – Learn how to grow your online presence using SEO.
3. DigitalMarketer.com – Learn about online marketing, tools, and training.
4. Bloggingtips.com – Learn how to start, grow, and monetize a blog.

PHOTOGRAPHY

Photography has changed throughout the years now that everyone has a high-powered camera in their pockets, but there will always be a need for certain photography gig work. The real estate market, for example, is highly dependent on great photos to increase the likelihood that a client will want to view listed properties in person. Wedding photography is still a good gig, although you'll have to stomach dealing with brides and their sometimes unrealistic expectations when in stressful situations.

Most people get into photography as a side hustle first and then reach a point where they eventually do it full time. Think about how you could stand out in a sea of photographers. Perhaps you only take photos of real estate. Perhaps you only take photos of theatre productions for a theatre company to use in their marketing. Perhaps you only take photos of newborn babies or even photos of pets. Both are huge markets ripe for the picking.

My friend Marie initially got into photography as a hobby but has since made a name for herself, photographing elopements in some of the most remote places in the United States. As she perfected her craft, she found a niche in elopement photography. Since she often wanted to shoot in locations that were hard to get to, she decided to go mobile and live out of a camper van. This allowed her to travel from location to location and capture some of the coolest and most unique pictures that I have ever seen.

Without expecting it, her business exploded. As her following grew, so did her leads—so much so that she had to recommend other elopement photography companies because she couldn't take them all. But if it weren't for the gig economy, she wouldn't be able to live and enjoy such a cool and freedom-granting lifestyle.

Photography is a great gig, but you'll have to find a niche or a way to stand out as Marie did. And if you successfully do find a niche that's underserved, be prepared to scale up!

SOFTWARE DEVELOPMENT

Software development is a big part of the gig economy and is also arguably one of the more lucrative ways to make a living working independently. If you have a background in coding or deep knowledge of how to manage, write, and work with software, you can find lots of gigs for big tech companies like Facebook and Google. When these companies build and release a new product, they often-times contract with a lot of freelance developers to work on the project. These gigs can range from three- to six- to twelve-month contracts. If you're impressive, you might be offered to jump to the next project once the current one is complete.

As a developer, you can also offer your services on websites like CodeMentor.io, a platform that breaks coding gigs up into fifteen-minute snippets. If someone is stuck on a bug in their code, they can fractionally hire developers to help them work through their specific issue. The transactions are quick and easy since they're set in fifteen-minute blocks, making it an easy way to earn good money in a short amount of time.

CONSULTING

Consulting is a great way to earn money in the gig economy. This is popular among gig workers who have become masters of their industry and who are well known in the circles in which they've worked. Consulting is also a go-to gig for retirees who no longer want to work a full-time job yet don't want to fully retire. Companies will hire consultants for continued access to the vast knowledge they've acquired throughout their careers and will pay them good money in return.

Say you're a part-time consultant with somewhat regular hours, maybe doing UX design. Your life doesn't look all that different from your more conventional co-workers if you don't want it to—but as a freelance consultant, you have control over your time in a way they don't. If you're working a fixed price contract and you're efficient, you've just given yourself a bonus. Even better, you won't have to sit through pointless meetings watching the clock. Instead, you'll probably be earning an hourly rate, so even if you do sit through countless meetings, you'll be earning a healthy living along the way.

I see a lot of consultants come from the corporate world.

My good friend's dad became a consultant after he retired from his executive role at a Fortune 500 company. Drawing on his long and vast experience, he now offers his advice and recommendations to companies on his own time. Consulting allows him the flexibility to balance his personal life with his work life, something he didn't have before.

THE SKY'S THE LIMIT

The list of jobs above is just a small collection of the most popular gigs; it is by no means a comprehensive list. If you can think of something that you're good at, there's probably a gig for it.

For example, a friend of mine, Alicia, is a professional dancer with a ballet company. In her free time, she teaches ballet to a handful of students, supplementing her income. Without having to sign up for an app, she opened herself up as a gig worker by charging for dance lessons. Even during the pandemic, she expanded her teaching business since the ballet company had to temporarily close down. Although she offers in-person lessons to her local community, with COVID-19, she also offers virtual lessons through ZOOM, which allows her to reach more people than she could before.

DO YOU HAVE WHAT IT TAKES?

The shift to gig work can give you freedom and control over

your time. It can free your energy to focus on the things you want. But if you're not careful, it can also spell disaster. Do you think you have what it takes? Let's find out in the next chapter.

CHAPTER FOUR

CAN YOU HANDLE THE GIG?

After talking to his friends and getting the lay of the land, Sam decided to go for it. He pictured himself walking out the door of his company and never looking back. He day-dreamed about being in charge of his own schedule and no longer working for the man.

It sounds so liberating, doesn't it?

A lot of people think this way at first, and I don't blame them. After all, I was once in their shoes. Once they realize what's happening in the gig economy, it sure seems like an attractive option. It's quite tempting to quit your day job and join the freelance world doing the first thing that sparks your interest.

The reality, however, is that the gig economy is not for everyone.

Yes, it can be a great place, but jumping in without a plan is like buying a house without setting aside funds for all the expenditures that will inevitably come up, like home repairs and property taxes—it's not wise or sustainable. It's like dating before you truly know yourself and what you want from a partner. When people come to me excited and eager to announce their impending leap, I fully support them but then make sure to tell them to do some groundwork first.

Success in the gig economy requires a lot of planning and foresight. Planning for your career in the gig economy begins long before you sign up to work with a service or start advertising your skills and talents on a freelance platform. First, you need to decide what kind of work will be the best fit for you.

Before you make any drastic decisions, you have to establish and understand your values, do your research, learn to stand out, and if you still haven't found your niche, start thinking outside the box.

GET PERSONAL

I encourage you to spend time doing a little soul-searching with the following questions. Answer them honestly. Taking a personal inventory like this provides you with a solid foundation from which to launch your gig life.

- What is most important to you in life? In other words, what are your values? Values are principles that drive you as a person, not just for work but for everyday living. For example, my values are integrity, character, reliability, consistency, loyalty, honesty, and open-mindedness.
- Do the projects or companies you're considering align with those values?
- What are you good at? Make a list. This will help guide your journey in searching for appropriate gigs.
- Is the work you're considering a good fit for you?
- What is your intention in getting into the gig economy? Are you looking to make extra money on the side or do gig work full time?
- If you take on new gig work, can you achieve balance between your family, personal, and work commitments?
- Are you ready to work hard?

Let's break down each of these questions.

PERSONAL VALUES EVOLVE

As time goes on, your answers to these questions might change, and that is okay. We must gain experience to learn what we do or don't want and how we best work. What was important to me five to ten years ago is not what's important to me now.

Your environment can influence your values, too. After I graduated from college, for example, money was a huge motivator for me. When you have no money as a broke college student, it naturally becomes a high priority. As I spent more time working and gaining experience, instead of chasing the high-dollar projects, I started leaning toward projects that appealed to me in other areas of life. These were projects that I could build into something sustainable and something that would help others in the long run. While I was first motivated solely by making money, the money quickly became a byproduct of what I was really doing: helping people.

Tip: People like working with those who share the same or similar values. This also means avoiding working with people with rotten values. I'm a member of a business networking group that focuses specifically on entrepreneurs, and whenever I have a particularly bad experience working with someone, I share that experience with the group, soliciting feedback to better my chances of identifying red flags when hiring in the future.

When it comes to values, keep in mind that your reputation is on the line. Freelancers who value money above all else, driven only by making a quick buck, will establish the reputation that they're only in it for the money. That reputation quickly spreads, and it'll be hard for them to get future work.

Life experiences can also hugely impact your values and how you see the world. It sure did for me. My mom was diagnosed with cancer while I was in college. She fought the cancer for a few years, and while I was motivated to make money with my side hustles during college, that money was also used to help pay for her medical bills and treatments. Since she wasn't working, I wanted to help provide a good quality of life for her as she battled her illness. Before she passed away a year after I graduated from college, working side gigs allowed me to spend time with her, which I am eternally grateful for.

Losing a parent changed me forever. It was a catalyst that helped my motivations mature from striving to simply make a bunch of money to instead focus on how I can use my skills to help people. It shaped my value system with regards to how I approach work and life to this day—including valuing time with family. I have three siblings; a twin brother and two younger sisters, as well as my dad. Because of my job, I'm able to spend a lot of time with them. Whether it's weekly family dinners, random trips together, or quality time one-on-one with each, the flexibility from my gig work allows me to almost never miss a family event.

Even if you think you know what your values are today, they might change over time—and oftentimes, that's for the better. Having said that, there are unintended consequences of uncertainty. For example, if you're steadily making good money and then all of a sudden you're not, your values might shift from helping others to survival mode, trying to keep your head above water. Keep your eyes open to constantly adapt to your surroundings. Things will change, but you need to know yourself.

As mentioned above, my values are integrity, character, reliability, consistency, loyalty, honesty, and open-mindedness. Because the gig economy is contract-based, I place integrity, honesty, and loyalty above everything else. This is mostly because I've done business with quite a few people in the past who tried to screw me over—some successfully doing so in the process.

These values have served me well, not only in attracting new leads and projects but in retaining them, too. When I first ventured out on my own, I'd casually offer my services to people for free, to be nice. Once word got around that I knew what I was doing, the floodgates of business were unleashed, and people started contacting me for paid consulting gigs.

When I'm hiring, I have a "no asshole" policy, and I look for the same values in candidates. Regardless of how talented a person *claims* to be, if they're going to be a pain to work with, I won't hire them. Throughout my interactions with contractors, I have frank conversations about expectations, and I wear my heart on my sleeve. I look at hiring as an opportunity to create a valuable relationship or partnership; I don't view it as a transaction. I tell them that I expect loyalty because I'm very loyal myself. I explain how I operate and then ask if they can operate in the same way. If they hesitate or say no, then we go our separate ways. I've used upwards of one hundred contractors over the years—whether through an agency or single independent freelancers—and those who have driven the most results are the ones who respect and trust me, and vice versa. The greedy and egotistical assholes who are just in it for a quick buck are *never* the ones that last long term. Their arrogance will almost always be their undoing.

A quick word of caution on contracts. Always have an attorney you trust look over your contracts or anything you sign. I've had both trusted clients and business partners weaponize the legal system against me, which ended up costing quite a bit of money as a result. In hindsight, I took those people at their word when they promised they wouldn't screw me over, so I didn't have an attorney look over the contracts before signing them. Now, however, I have an attorney look over every single contract, no matter how close I am with the person I am entering into the contract with. Business is business, and you can never be too careful.

Your personality can drive your values, too. I've always been an internally driven person. It is none of my business what other people think of me or my work. If I achieve a goal, I do so for myself, not for the validation that comes from others seeing my achievements and giving me praise. If I get recognized along the way, that's nice and certainly a perk, but I am not driven by accolades or being featured in a magazine. My drive for success comes purely from within.

Some people do well working for others. They like supervision and enjoy checking off a laundry list of things that were put together by someone else. They like being told exactly what to build and precisely how to build it. I am not one of those people—but I didn't learn this until I'd spent some time in the field working.

When I first got out on my own, to supplement my income while my projects were gaining traction, I took on contract work for others. Since I was good at building websites, I started designing websites for other people. In my mind, it seemed easy enough, but I soon found out that I did not enjoy working for others.

After designing my third website or so, I realized that designing websites for others was not the same as designing websites for myself. When working for myself, I approve things instantly, constantly reset expectations based on how my work is going, and have a firm understanding of what I'm doing.

While designing websites for others, however, I realized

that they oftentimes do not have the same ability to pivot or see things differently. I got frustrated working on somebody else's projects because I was limited in what I could do under their supervision. While I got to design a really cool website and get paid for doing so, the downside was they got to reap the rewards of having an excellent website, and I was sent off to do it again for someone else.

This made me want to work solely for myself even more so I could own the websites I built. I know there are a lot of people who don't want to take that risk, that they're okay with building things for other people, and that's great. I just happen to be a long-term strategic thinker who doesn't want to be constantly chasing contracts. I'm also someone who can stomach losing, overnight and without warning, 30 percent of the traffic and revenue to one of my sites. Not everyone feels comfortable with that.

Another reason the consulting gig was short-lived was because people took advantage of me. I'd give them an inch, and they'd take twenty miles. Frustrated and fed up, I quickly decided that I was done working for others, so I focused on running my own businesses—and I haven't strayed from that promise to myself since then. When people want me to work for them, I politely decline.

Staying disciplined and laser-focused on my values has allowed me to find success in building really big, cool stuff.

Of those projects, Gigworker.com, is one. Had I gone the consulting route, I would not have had the time to grow the site into what it is today. I'd be busy building somebody else's dream instead of my own.

RESEARCH COMPANY VALUES

If you're pursuing work through an app-based platform, take the time to research the company's values and see if they match with yours. I didn't do this when I first drove for Uber, and I wish I had.

Back when ridesharing was new and growing, I joined both Uber and Lyft as a driver. Lyft marketed itself as "Your Friend with a Car;" Uber did not. Uber's approach was more cutthroat. When I started Ridester.com as the go-to site for information regarding all ridesharing topics and companies, I worked with both companies to make sure everything I published was accurate. I had contacts at the corporate offices of both companies, and they would often communicate if something on my website was incorrect. If there was a problem with Lyft, one of their representatives would kindly email me and ask to rectify the situation. Whether that was modifying an article or updating a page, they were always patient and very reasonable in their requests. Uber, on the other hand, was a bit more aggressive. Unlike Lyft, Uber would threaten legal action or shut me out of their referral programs entirely until the issue was addressed.

Clearly, it was frustrating to work with Uber and the strong-arm tactics they used. It seemed like Lyft actually cared about their drivers and their partners. Uber, not so much. To give Uber credit, though, things have greatly improved over the years under the leadership of their new CEO, and working with them is now enjoyable.

Most companies these days have a value statement that they publicly share online. If they don't, their values are pretty obvious if you do a little research. Look through their website. Scroll through the comments on their social media accounts. Review what previous employees are writing about the company on websites like Glassdoor.com or Indeed.com. You can get a pretty good idea of the company's values by how they interact with the public.

It's not just about app-based gigs or brokers, either. If you're a freelancer, you want to vet your clients, too. Some clients are just not worth the effort. Maybe your personalities will clash, which will take up much of your time, energy, and sanity. Over time, this will suck the life out of you and drain you of your entrepreneurial energy.

When I first started Gigworker, I hired a freelance "strategy consultant" that seemed to know what he was doing. He said all the right things and even appeared to be a perfect fit for his role—helping to build out a team to help me scale a software platform that matched gig workers with gigs.

However, the downside was that his skillset did not live up to his talk. He constantly wanted me to be on calls and in meetings with him—ones that I had no reason to join. He talked about ideas to implement but was unable to actually execute those ideas and bring them to life.

When I wasn't in the office, he would incessantly call me just to talk. It seemed like he just couldn't function without me, no matter what time of day or night, and that got in the way of the things that I needed to accomplish. It got to the point that the meetings and calls were taking up the majority of my days, evenings, and nights, and I wasn't getting much of my own work done—let alone having a personal life outside of work.

With time, it became clear that he really had no idea what he was doing. He could talk the talk, but when it came time to produce results, he fell flat and outright failed in every way. He also developed a huge ego because he was part of something that was growing—but not because of his own work.

Additionally, he constantly stirred up needless drama without cause. Simply put, he thrived in chaos. After dealing with this ever-increasing neediness, drama, and utter lack of results, I cut him loose and reclaimed my independence.

Since parting ways with him, my life has been fairly drama-free, and I've gotten back to actually getting things done and moving the business forward.

These are the projects from hell that are difficult to deal with. When it comes to freelancing, don't underestimate your gut. Humans are pretty intuitive when it comes to other people. Once you know the values that drive you, it's easy to see and connect with people who share those values, even if you don't explicitly talk about them. If I had stuck to my values and not compromised on them to hire this particular consultant, I would have saved a year of my life and endured far less chaos, all while getting things done.

If you want fulfillment out of the work you do, try to find a company that identifies with your values. Otherwise, you're going to get really frustrated.

WHAT ARE YOU GOOD AT?

This might seem obvious, and it is in a way, but it's not just limited to skills like writing, editing, photography, or development. Are you good at big picture analysis, or are you good at strategy? Say you have an MBA and excel at identifying patterns and trends; perhaps someone from the restaurant industry would hire you to help them enter a new market. If you excel at interpersonal communication and networking, a brand might hire you to fix their local image. List the obvious talents that you're good at, but think beyond them as well.

Before I joined the gig economy, making my own list was a challenge for me. I spent the majority of my life—whether through academics, sports, or other extracurricular activities—in the middle of the pack. I wasn't outstanding, but I wasn't absolutely horrible, either. I made the varsity basketball team in high school, but I wasn't the star player. I would complete work during my college internships, but my work didn't receive much praise from my boss. It wasn't until gig work that I really hit my stride and found my passion—and it's definitely not working for corporate America. My mind is wired to think outside the box and far outside the constraints of somebody else's vision.

So what am I good at? I'm good at seeing opportunities and monetizing them. I'm good with discipline, which helps me research those opportunities and act on them. I'm good at problem-solving. I can work through most problems in my head, finding the most effective and efficient solutions. I am also not afraid of hard work or long hours, and I possess the motivation to actually do the work. And when things get tough, I have the grit to work through things without losing motivation and giving up.

There's a common term used to describe those who talk the talk but don't walk the walk: *wantrepreneur*. If someone wants to be creative and contribute to the world, but they get turned off by the amount of energy and effort it's going to take, they don't actually do anything. Instead, they just keep talking about what they want to achieve. That's a *wantrepreneur*. They're "ideas" people but not "shovels in the ground" people. They like to talk about how their idea is going to make a lot of money, but they don't actually pull the trigger on it. Consequently, they'll never make much money taking that route.

I am the exact opposite. I'm good at committing to ideas and doing whatever necessary to get them off the ground. And by default, I don't give up easily. If I see an opportunity, and if it makes sense, I'll go after it and keep at it until it works.

Tip: Find your passion. The great thing about a passion is that it doesn't fade with time. If anything, it gets stronger. When you're good at what you're passionate about, you'll find it easier to get up and tackle each day. All the things I was passionate about at the start of my journey are still things I'm passionate about today.

ARE YOU A GOOD FIT?

When you want to evaluate if something's a good fit, the best thing to do is test your idea.

Although leaving the job I had working for my dad was the hardest decision I've ever made, I didn't just dive into the deep end of my current gig all at once. I had data under my belt since I spent years testing my website. After validating that my ideas worked, it was then a matter of whether or not I could scale the thing. I knew it was a good fit because I tested the waters on a part-time basis while still working my day job full time, which allowed the project to generate an income before quitting my job and diving all in.

Working in the gig economy isn't like working in an office setting where you see the same people over and over again. Gig work can often be lonely and isolating, so if you don't know how to cope with that, start thinking about what you need in order to be social (more on this in Chapter Six). This was really hard for me at first. Being on your own forces you to focus for long hours at a time and deeply work in order to support yourself. That can also be incredibly stressful, and I didn't have many people to talk with about that struggle. It almost became a taboo topic with my family and friends because they didn't really understand. This was my choice, after all. I shouldn't complain—but it's worth noting, if you're a contractor or an employee for a company, regardless of the industry you're in, you can expect to encounter stresses in your job. This was something I struggled with at first, but now it's normal, and I have no problem with it.

Are you good with money? Are you a saver, or are you a spender? If you're not good with finances, gig work may not be for you. With a full-time job, you have the predictability of a steady paycheck, so you can plan accordingly every month. When you're working for yourself, however, you might have a week or month where you don't make any income whatsoever, so how do you deal with that? You have to plan for it. You have to accumulate a rainy-day fund. You have to minimize your debt and live within your means.

When Ridester was pulling in a good amount of money from Uber and my pool of clients when I first started, I felt like I was on cloud nine. I successfully managed to support myself—making more money than ever before. Naturally, I grew overconfident and started acting as such. I started traveling and checking things off of my bucket list at a record clip. I was living the dream.

At the time, I made a good chunk of change from Uber's referral program every month. It was one of the largest revenue streams from my website. I was invited to Arizona for a friend's bachelor party but decided to fly down a few days prior to relax by the pool and work on my tan. As I sat down with a cup of coffee and opened my laptop, I checked my email and learned that without notice, Uber had shut down their driver referral program, and the income from that part of the site instantly vanished. I started to freak out and called my contacts at Uber. After a little back and forth, it became clear that their incentive program was eliminated entirely and wasn't coming back.

As I sat there stunned, I looked around at the nice hotel and the glassy water in the pool. That's when it hit me: all of this money, freedom, and flexibility could go away if I wasn't careful. Sure, I had other sources of income, but what if that all went away, too? The thought of losing it all made me realize that I had to be smarter with my spending habits, which included lavish traveling.

That's when I stopped being so frivolous with my money and restricted my traveling to be more purposeful and planned. I started to treat all of my work as if everything could come crashing down on me the next day. Nothing was guaranteed. Now, in everything I do, I plan for the worst and hope for the best. If something goes away, I'm not caught off guard by any surprises, and if it continues going well, then that's just cake for me.

Be careful of lifestyle creep as well. Some people, when they increase their income, increase their spending accordingly. This happened to a buddy of mine. He drove a Honda Accord, but after he landed a couple of contracts worth $80,000, he rushed out and leased a brand-new Range Rover. Unfortunately, one of the contracts didn't work out, and he was forced to trade in that Range Rover for another modest, less expensive family vehicle.

My wake-up call in Arizona allowed me to avoid this lifestyle creep over the long run. I was caught up in it for a second but thankfully managed to do an about-face before it bit me in the butt.

Do you consider yourself an independent person? I mean this in the broadest of ways. The nine-to-five culture is so ingrained in some people that they can't work outside that box. When you're working on your own, having full control of scheduling, work, and pay sounds dreamy, but you're taking on extra responsibilities and independence that you might not think about right away. There is no such thing as paid sick days or PTO in the gig economy. You are responsible for taking care of yourself, including your finances, even when you can't work.

But there are obvious advantages to this independence, too—so long as you can adequately plan ahead. At a full-time job, if you need to take your dog to the vet, you have to request time off from work. You may not be paid for that time off, or you'll be forced to use one of your limited PTO days. When you work for yourself, you can take your dog to the next available appointment and then work late that night. For instance, when I made an appointment to get LASIK eye surgery, I made it for the soonest available time and then worked until midnight in the days leading up to the surgery. Since the recovery takes a few days, I preloaded my work so I could take those days off without it negatively affecting the things I needed to get done. If you can't think ahead and plan accordingly for situations like these, gig work may not be a good fit.

The same can be said for vacation. Although you can take a vacation anytime you want, you'll need to plan ahead to make sure you can take time off without negatively affecting your income, your projects, or your relationships. Most gig workers I know end up working on their vacations to some degree. Are you okay with that? If you're not, that's fine, but then you might need to work more beforehand or work extra after you come back to make up for any lost revenue. The same can be said for health insurance and retirement accounts. You'll have to do your own research to find what best suits you and then pay into those accounts on your own.

Are you the type of person that can do these things on your own? Or do you prefer working for a company that handles them for you? If it's the latter, you might not be a good fit.

The most successful gig workers tend to be most passionate about the lifestyle benefits. If you're not attracted to working in one location for the majority of the year, then gig life may be a great fit. If you'd rather have flexibility than a big paycheck, gig life may be good for you, too. For many, lifestyle is the reason they got into independent work in the first place; in fact, 84 percent of gig workers say they consciously prioritize lifestyle over earnings. And they're acting on those priorities: 85 percent of freelancers value being able to move to an area that caters to their lifestyle, and they can do it because they don't need to live near a traditional employer.[17] No need to live in Manhattan if you're the wide-open spaces type, and vice versa.

When you work for yourself, you're not forced to be somewhere at eight o'clock in the morning ready to tackle the day. Perhaps you're the type who does their best work from seven o'clock to eleven o'clock in the evening and sleeps in until ten o'clock in the morning. Perhaps you're a surfer and want to catch the morning waves before the crowds, so you make your work schedule fit that lifestyle. If you are disciplined enough to put in the work while living your preferred lifestyle, then gig work may be a great fit for you.

WHAT IS YOUR INTENTION?

What is your intention with the gig economy? Are you looking to make extra money on the side or do gig work full-time? The answer to this question will vary for each individual, but it is important to understand because it will heavily influence how you will achieve your vision and goals.

For example, if you plan on doing some freelance editing on a part-time level, you'll want to avoid any full-time gigs.

---

17   https://www.slideshare.net/upwork/freelancing-in-america-2018-120288770/1.

This may seem obvious, but I can't tell you how many times people underestimate the time it takes to work on a project, and then suddenly, they're stuck working two full-time jobs, stressing out like crazy, and finding zero work-life balance. Even worse is if they're not getting paid what they're worth on such projects. Trust me when I say that you don't want this to happen to you.

Set boundaries for yourself, recognize the type of work that fits your schedule and don't bid on projects that you can't handle in your current situation.

Whenever I use Uber, I take the opportunity to ask the driver some questions about why he or she is driving. Most of the time, I get the typical, "This is my full-time gig," or, "This is my part-time gig to make some extra money in my spare time." Everyone has a different reason for driving, but one driver's story stood out to me the most. He was a man in his forties who apparently made a great deal of money after selling his business, only to start a program that mentors young adults about business and life. He drove for Uber as a way to make extra money that he used to throw pizza parties and other fun events for the kids. I'm willing to bet that one of his values was altruism, and his intention was to make money on a part-time basis to support his mentorship program.

COMMON REASONS PEOPLE ENTER THE GIG

1. To make extra money.
2. To expand a hobby they enjoy doing.
3. To bridge the gap between their full-time job and their freelance job, in hopes to eventually go full-time with their freelance job.
4. To supplement their savings or retirement, or help with extra costs.
5. To find more fulfillment in their life.

PERSONAL RELATIONSHIPS CHANGE

Your personal relationships with the ones you love will likely change once you make the plunge into the gig economy. This is something that many people overlook. They jump into the gig economy with such fortitude, thinking, "I need to make a certain amount of money, or I need to get that contract." People can be so focused on the gig, they tend to become workaholics and forget about their family and friends. Failure to find that balance then leads to frustration with family, spouses, and sometimes even friends.

I dated a great girl back when I worked for my dad's company and started dabbling with gig work. She subscribed to the mentality that after college, you're supposed to work a nine to five at some huge, stable corporation with decent pay and great benefits. Meanwhile, I was working more than sixty hours per week at my full-time job, on top of hours and hours of gig work. That did not sit well with her, to say the least. The more I worked on my gigs, the less time I had for her. She didn't understand the long-term goals I had in mind: I wanted to front-load the work while I was young so that I didn't have to work as much later in life when we had a family. Our relationship suffered since our values and expectations were different. I wanted to please her, but I also wanted to continue building my side hustle and exploring additional ways to make money on my own terms. Since I was still so new to gig work, she made me question my decision—enough that I even considered selling Ridester and getting a job in the corporate world.

Thankfully, that never happened. We broke up a year later and I kept working on the website. Now, I can confidently look back and say, had I gone through with the sale, that would have been the worst decision I would ever make in my life. My career in the gig economy would have likely ended there.

In retrospect, I did work a lot, but this was during my mom's battle with cancer. When she passed away, it forced me to grow up very quickly. I went from that college mentality of living in the moment to a mentality of, "What are we on earth for?" Needless to say, that didn't happen to my girlfriend. Our value systems clashed, and we went our separate ways.

I place a lot of value on experiences over material things. I grew up and still live in Omaha, Nebraska. People in Omaha tend to subscribe to the same mentality of complacency: they find a nine-to-five corporate job with good pay and benefits; they get married in their early twenties; shortly thereafter, they start having kids. Many never even get the chance to travel or explore the world.

There's certainly nothing wrong with that, but the life that came with settling down so young didn't match my immediate goals. What the gig economy has allowed me to do instead is travel the world and create meaningful experiences doing interesting things with cool people. And the more I travel, the more I want to continue doing so. I've created a life that allows me to support myself, balance my priorities, *and* travel—which is hard for some to fathom.

They say we are most like the five or six people we are closest to, so if all of your buddies are on the corporate career path, then it might be hard for you to break out of that thinking. And when you do, don't be surprised if your friends give you a hard time about your choice. Those who have never done gig work might not understand the appeal. They might be jealous and then lash out in unexpected ways. They might belittle you, thinking you don't put in the hours as they do. If they react negatively, that's only because they don't know what they don't know. Don't let them hold you back from creating the life that you want because they can't see your vision.

BE PREPARED TO WORK HARD

Working hard is always a part of the equation. You can't expect not to work hard. The gig economy is the epitome of the common saying, "You have to work hard in order to play hard."

In early February, I went on a scuba diving trip to the Turks and Caicos Islands and spent a week diving with sharks and humpback whales. Sounds amazing, right? But the three weeks leading up to that trip, I worked fourteen- to eighteen-hour days in order to get all my work done before the trip.

Working in the gig economy is often romanticized. You get to travel. You can take time off whenever you feel like it. You get to do whatever you want. This is true, but I still have to put in the work in order to do those things. I just don't have to get my vacation approved by someone "above" me.

In the beginning, it's going to seem hard and frustrating. This is normal. The learning curve can be significant, depending on your level of experience and what you're venturing out to do. But the more time you spend in the field making contacts, building relationships, submitting bids, and completing work, the easier everything will become.

I used to spend hours learning about building and monetizing websites. I watched countless videos and read even more articles and books. My learning curve was astonishingly massive. I didn't know what would work or what would fail, and the only way to find out was through trial and error. After years of practice, I've learned to become much more efficient, and my work has become second nature. The same will happen to you. The more time you spend on your craft, the more you'll learn how to improve it. You'll be more efficient and more productive. But expect to work hard, especially in the beginning.

And what about that elusive "work-life balance" everyone seems to always be chasing? It's definitely possible, but it will still take hard work.

For me, it took about two years to get to a point where I could say I found balance. It clicked once I spent enough time in my industry to understand the minute intricacies of how to be more efficient. This meant spending less time on the work yet still producing the same high-level quality. I was working smarter, not just harder. I then figured out how much work I needed to pay my expenses and live a lifestyle that I'm happy with. I want to travel, so how many gigs do I need to take on in order to do that? When all of that clicked in my mind, that's when I started prioritizing friendships and relationships over my work, and that's when I found work-life balance.

If you think you have what it takes to join the gig economy after digging deep and getting personal, your next step is to dive in. In the next chapter, we'll talk about how to get in on the gig and how to be successful while doing so.

CHAPTER FIVE

GETTING IN ON THE GIG...AND SUCCEEDING

"I can't wait to go to work every day!"

I hear these words all the time from people who have made the shift to gig work. They don't love everything about it, of course, but they do love being able to choose what they do and when they do it, rather than forcing themselves into a pre-defined role and schedule. Back when they worked a job like that, they faced each day in a very different frame of mind.

Now that they've switched, they're astonished to discover how much better they feel. That satisfaction often starts with discovering how efficient they can be now that they don't have to deal with the conventional schedule set by many traditional jobs. When I started working independently, I got more done working two hours for myself than I could in eight hours working for someone else. I have control over my time and fewer distractions; not only does that make the work day more pleasant, it means I can make more money because I can work on things that drive revenue for my business.

While independent work isn't a get-rich-quick solution (see Chapter Three), you *can* reap greater financial rewards than you would in a conventional job because you're no longer working under a salary cap. Now your earning potential is theoretically limited only by your commitment and the time you have available. You don't have to spend every day making the boss rich. You're the boss now; if you excel, you're going to be rewarded.

When you work for yourself, you have freedom with your time. What can you do with that freedom? Full-time work is limiting, and gig work is not. With freedom, you open yourself up to more opportunities. Personally, this freedom has given me more confidence in myself. Sure, traveling anywhere, meeting new people, and learning about other cultures are rewarding, but the unexpected benefit is chasing opportunities for growth. That freedom gives you the ability to do what you want, but it's also deeper than that. You can really find yourself. You have the ability to figure out what you truly want in life.

Personally, I don't want to be tied down to one place. I want to experience life to the fullest. The more I explore the world, the more confident I become. It's a cycle that compounds on itself. Because I want to travel more, I work harder on my business, and the better it goes, the more confident I get. The more successful the businesses, the more I can travel, the more I can scale it and outsource it. It's a full circle that keeps feeding on itself.

So how do you get started?

THE BEGINNING IS ALWAYS THE HARDEST

Now that you've defined your values and goals, how do you find a job that's right for you? If you're like most people, you type something like "part-time graphic design jobs" into Google and try to cope with the deluge of results that follows. It can be a real slog; the gig economy has grown so big and so fast that most people spend an inordinate amount of time flailing around the internet looking for a starting point.

Or, if they have a specific field in mind, they might visit online marketplaces such as Freelancer.com, or create an account on Fiverr, UpWork, or any number of gig marketplaces (I, of course, personally recommend Gigworker. com). This approach can be useful since there are enough gigs posted that most people will eventually land on something that is a good fit. But this approach can also be painful because there are so many hoops to jump through.

After you sign up for one of these marketplaces, answer the profile questions, and post a portfolio, you're finally ready to start responding to gig requests with carefully crafted pitches, most of which will go nowhere at first. Don't give up. As you gain more and more experience, you will do better and better at winning bids.

Tip: Be authentic. Some freelancers make the mistake of fluffing up their experience in order to get work, and I must caution you away from doing that. Just be you. Be authentic. I prefer hiring solo freelancers as opposed to using an agency because many agencies will say that they have a lot of experience and that they're good at everything. But when it comes down to it, they don't produce the results I initially want, which leads to wasted money. Meanwhile, I could have hired a freelancer with no clout who is very focused on just one area but excels in that work.

There's a guy in my office who is really good at social media. He has no problem sharing what he knows with anyone who cares to listen—and he does this out of the goodness of his heart. He's not trying to sell himself or claim he's the best or that he should be hired by whomever he is talking to. He freely shares his knowledge because he genuinely wants to help.

I liken getting gigs to dating: don't try too hard. If you try too hard to impress the person you're interested in, they can smell that from a mile away and won't be interested. But if you're comfortable in your own skin and let your personality come through authentically and naturally, then people are more open to receiving you organically. It's the same in the gig economy. Let your work and skillset speak for themselves. You don't have to embellish or put yourself on a pedestal to get hired. Just be your authentic and honest self, and the pieces will fall into place.

The more work you do, the better you'll get. The more you practice bidding, the better you'll become. And the more experience you gain, the better you'll become at knowing your worth and what to charge.

Unfortunately, most job seekers don't do a comprehensive search or even hop on a job board. Instead, they start with names they've heard before, such as Airbnb or Uber. That might work out fine for them, but it means they're only exploring one small corner of the gig economy. Chances are, they've never considered transcribing videos or teaching English online, or any of the other gigs that might be a better fit, because they don't even know about them.

Finding and vetting gigs has been a frustrating and time-consuming struggle for a long time because nobody has built a reliable, comprehensive resource. Instead, the internet is filled with fractional players in the game trying to do their best at solving their own piece of the puzzle. The gig economy is a segmented, siloed industry. There are job boards for applying for jobs, like FlexJobs.com, but those job boards don't tell you which services and products you need to excel. There are online training platforms, like Udemy.com, but those platforms don't provide you with a way to apply for jobs similar to what you're getting trained for. And don't even get me started on the lack of helpful and up-to-date information about the gig economy.

What if there was a resource that included all of those resources together?

With Gigworker.com, we're looking to change that. We have created a research center, a one-stop-shop to help people explore the gig work terrain without getting overwhelmed. At Gigworker.com, we maintain an exhaustive, current collection of resources for independent workers, and we customize results to meet the searcher's needs. In other words, we're searching for everything, but you only have to see the results that matter to you. We think of ourselves as a college career counselor but for everyone and for the gig economy.

Gigworker has it all. It's not just about finding jobs and applying for them. It's not just about elevating your skills to do that job well. We also provide lifestyle tips on how to succeed as a gig worker. If you're working from home, we'll provide best practices on how to organize your time. We have a robust job board where you can search for gigs, and we'll recommend product services training to help you excel in those roles. It's a one-stop shop regardless of where you're at in the process.

RESEARCH THE COST OF DOING BUSINESS

My old roommate signed up for Uber to drive on the weekends for extra money, but he didn't research how much he'd also be putting into the job. When accepting rides, he wouldn't factor in the distance versus the amount he would get paid. He'd just get in his car and accept work with no further thought. In his eyes, he was making money the whole time. On some rides, he could net $10, but there were other rides where he only cleared $1.

A part of doing your research is also figuring out what the cost of doing business will be. In other words, how much are you spending to bring in money? A lot of people don't take this into consideration when deciding to pursue work in the gig economy—especially at the lower level of task-oriented jobs, such as dog walking, house sitting, or Uber driving. They might be excited to make that extra $20, but how much time did they invest to earn it? Was it worth it?

In the case of my old Uber-driving roommate, to get that

$10 ride, he'd drive thirty minutes across town, overlooking the dead miles, gas, and deprecation he was putting on his vehicle in the process. This simple mistake likely led to tens of hours of downtime, hundreds of dollars of wasted gas, and more wear and tear on his vehicle than he would've liked. Take a month's worth of inefficiencies, multiply them by twelve, and you start to see how powerful this concept becomes.

Investing four hours to make twenty dollars isn't nearly as effective as working for an employer at fifteen dollars an hour. This is why I encourage you to do your research and think through the financial part of your decision.

Also, be wary of spending money on subscriptions, tools, and software that may benefit your business in the long run but aren't quite necessary at the present moment. I personally fell into this trap. Early on, I spent thousands of dollars on tools to research content for my website without even having a website built yet. I got excited and jumped the gun on something before I actually needed it. These tools were eventually helpful later, but I could have initially saved myself some money by focusing on what I needed to do at that moment in time instead of trying to do it all at once.

The key takeaway here is for you to learn the job before you start spending money on the job.

UNDERSTAND THE GIG CYCLE

App-based platform companies tend to follow a predictable cycle, offering different types of opportunities at different stages. Before you start applying for gigs, it pays to get a sense of each company's evolution in order to discover what stage they're in at the time you are considering applying. There are four main stages: market assessment and entry, supply acquisition, demand growth, and operational sustainability.

MARKET ASSESSMENT AND ENTRY

When a gig platform such as Uber, Lyft, Airbnb, or even Upwork launches, they start by evaluating new territories for market fit and growth potential. They analyze locations for expansion and determine how a new market will contribute to the bottom line. When assessing a new app-based service, you want to ask yourself a few questions. Will customers be interested in this service? Do they need it? Will this service work in your location? Are there enough potential workers in the area to make the service work?

A boat rental company, for example, probably wouldn't come to land-locked Nebraska since there aren't a lot of places to use a boat. The company would be better off opening in Boston or Minnesota. In such cities with lakes, the company is more likely to have enough users interested in renting a boat to actually make the service work.

During this stage, there may not be many positions for gig workers, but if you can find out what's going on, you'll be ready to raise your hand when the next, more opportunity-filled stage begins.

SUPPLY ACQUISITION

In the supply acquisition stage, companies start hiring gig workers. This is an ideal time to jump in because companies are usually willing to spend a great deal of money to establish themselves. In the early stages of their operations in Omaha, Lyft once offered a $1,000 earning guarantee: new drivers who gave 125 rides in the first ninety days were guaranteed a payout of $1,000 for those rides. If the income from those rides didn't add up to at least $1,000, the company would make up the difference. They wanted drivers on the road, and they were willing to pay for it because, at the most basic level, without drivers, they didn't have a platform. They need you, and they know it, so leverage this stage as much as possible.

DEMAND GROWTH

Once a company has validated the market and brought on workers, they begin spending money on advertising. Rideshare services might give away free credit to riders to encourage them to use the platform. Airbnb might offer credit when an existing user refers to a friend. Udemy might offer discounted courses for freelancers when they sign up using a friend's link, and so on. For more examples of this, see Chapter One again. Any company's growth stage is a great time to get involved because your services will be needed more than ever.

OPERATIONAL SUSTAINABILITY

Eventually, supply and demand are both met, and the gig company enters a period of stability. Uber and Lyft, for example, have millions of people now using their platforms and plenty of drivers to serve them. The bad news for you: as the gold rush winds down, prices are likely going to drop, and so will your pay as a result. You're unlikely to receive huge bonuses at this stage, and the company may even start taking bigger fees out of your paychecks. The good news: your hours may become more predictable, making your schedule more manageable and consistent.

The reason these companies drop prices in the operational sustainability phase is so that they can work towards making a profit. There is a huge push for this stage, especially once the company has gained market share because the venture capitalists that backed these well-funded companies need to make back their investment and turn a profit.

If you understand this cycle, you can ride the wave. Lots of people do this—they keep their original gig, but they jump on the newcomers, too. I know plenty of people who were happy driving for Lyft, but when Via came to town, they supplemented their income with that because Via was offering 30 percent higher pay. One of the reasons I started Gigworker.com was to help people navigate this cycle by staying on top of what's going on.

STAND OUT FROM THE COMPETITION

With more and more people joining the gig economy year after year, competition can be stiff. Consider some numbers from Upwork: midway through 2019, they had 2.02 million workers registered on the site, up from 1.72 million just a year earlier. The number of gigs posted, on the other hand, grew only modestly, from sixty-nine thousand to seventy-six thousand.[18] Competition is fierce and only getting fiercer.

Businesses are not jumping into the gig economy as fast, meaning there will be more people competing for work, but work is not being added as quickly to match. Most companies still hire people as employees as opposed to contractors. As such, the demand for gigs is outpacing the supply of them.

It's what happened during the California Gold Rush. There were more miners than there was gold, but men still trav-

---

18   https://media.thinknum.com/articles/gig-economy-slowdown-on-upwork/.

eled to those hills in hopes of finding fortune. The handful who were resilient and invested the time and money required to succeed came out rich. The majority of people, however, got left in the dust. That's what's happening now, and it's only going to get worse with advancements in efficiencies like automation.

Automation, particularly as it relates to artificial intelligence, will drastically change our world, including work in the gig economy. On the surface, automation will affect transactional workers like Uber drivers. With self-driving cars, rideshare drivers will no longer be necessary. Human capital will be replaced with options that cost far less than a human driver. This will also disrupt transportation for truckers and delivery drivers. But if you look deeper, technological advancements will go much further than that, with AI eventually replacing skills like writing and editing. We currently have software like Grammarly that will check grammar as you respond to emails, write an essay for school, or even write a complete book with a little guidance. There are already computers that can put together language, even poetry, and with enough time and improvements to the software, eventually, you won't be able to tell the difference.

Back in the 1990s, the Adobe Creative Suite, which includes programs like Photoshop, InDesign, and Illustrator, was exorbitantly expensive. But thanks to today's technology, those programs are now available in the cloud, where anyone can pay a fraction of the cost they once did and download these programs straight to their computer. With this type of inexpensive and widespread access, more people have developed the skills needed to work with such programs, so that skillset isn't as valuable as it once was.

The same thing happened with photography. Cameras and hardware are cheaper than ever, thanks to today's digital options. And now that all of our phones have cameras that are beginning to rival expensive DSLR cameras, well, everyone's a photographer. High-quality videos are made on iPhones these days. Even just five years ago, we didn't think this type of quality was achievable on a smartphone.

Design work will head toward automation, too. Even now, Microsoft's PowerPoint has an AI feature that suggests designs for you to pick, based on the content you place on the slides. Professional designers might scoff at this at first, but these AI designs are actually pretty impressive, especially for the price tag.

As automation increases and barriers to entry decrease, so will competition because the people displaced by automation are going to be looking for work, and it will be easier than ever to start a gig. They might find a job working for a corporation or big business, or they're going to enter the gig economy, or both, which means more people will be placing bids on the same projects, even though they might not have the skills to do the work.

You might think this future looks bleak, but success all boils down to how you position yourself as a gig worker. You can stand out in areas where computers can't grasp, like high-level strategy and vision. While computers can do millions of calculations a second, when it comes to distinguishing things like ethics and integrity, they fall flat. They're just not capable of that yet, and who knows if they'll ever be.

Don't let this discourage you. However, there is an impending sense of urgency. Get in before automation increases and pay attention to the changes. These changes won't happen overnight, but at the same time, technology moves quickly enough that you can't risk getting left behind.

Another unexpected influx of people flooding the gig market is due to the effects of COVID-19. The pandemic of 2020 pushed a lot of people into the gig economy. With more than forty million people applying for unemployment in the three months after the country's shutdown, how many of them do you think will turn to gig work to help make ends meet?

I'm guessing a lot.

Once you have defined your goals and chosen opportunities to pursue, your next challenge is to find a way to stand out from the crowd. When I started out as an Uber driver, competition for time behind the wheel was virtually non-existent—Uber couldn't get enough drivers, so they were courting workers with huge bonuses and incentives. Today, it's a different world.

People new to gig work often think they can simply sign up with a gig company, and they'll automatically get a list of gigs they can go do. It doesn't work that way. You have to sell yourself and be smart. Pay attention to the details when you apply, and when you begin the gig. Don't be the person who signs up on Rover and fails to fully fill out your profile, then wonders why nobody contacts you. Chances are, someone else better understands the social optics that are necessary to win gigs, and their profile is full of pictures of them with dogs on their lap or having a great time with their furry friends. Those are the people I hire when trying to find a sitter or walker for my dog. If they put in the time to craft an appealing profile, they'll probably go the extra mile while watching my dog.

The gig economy also heavily depends on two-sided reviews. Peer reviews are a way to filter out poor workers and elevate good ones. The better reviews you have, the more work you're going to get. Starting out initially can be challenging since you'll have to get creative in how you stand out to get jobs in order for them to later review you. But once you've done a few gigs, be sure to ask for reviews.

One of the big keys to gig economy success is finding something that you love and are good at, but arguably even more important is perception. Keeping in mind that there are oftentimes tens if not hundreds of gig workers bidding on the same project, so communicating your skills and being perceived by the client as the best fit for the gig is a must. Perception is key to winning bids and retaining clients. And although marketing yourself is important, what I mean by perception is putting yourself in the shoes of someone looking to hire you. How do they see you? What would they think of you?

Take some time to think about what customers are looking for and how you can stand out. It comes down to one question: If you were in their shoes looking for a gig worker, would you pick you?

That's why it's important to stand out from the competition because if you don't, anyone can take your place—whether they're good or not. And considering what happened with COVID-19, there will be more people looking for jobs in general, many of whom will likely turn to gig work as a result. Consider exploring one or all of the following to help you stand out: complete certifications and/or skills tests, adopt a learning mindset, beware of scammers, and stay on top of updates.

CERTIFICATIONS AND SKILLS TESTS

The gig economy is largely based on the review system, but as time goes on and we see more structure, certifications and skill tests are going to become increasingly important. One way to distinguish yourself is to get certified in your area of expertise, so potential employers have proof of your skills. Regardless of your field—software developers, event planners, life coaches, copyeditors, data analysts, and so on—there is likely a certification or skills test that you can take. Getting certified can be a significant investment both in time and money, depending on your field, but it can make a big difference.

More and more websites like Fiverr and FlexJobs now offer various skills tests users can take to establish credibility in their fields. These skills tests will help differentiate you to potential employers when they're looking for help on a project.

And these skills tests are usually pretty difficult, for good reason. They want to connect the companies using their sites with workers who have the appropriate level of skill to complete the gigs they are bidding on. Say you're a video editor looking for a job on Fiverr. You can take a skills test that will publicly show your competency in that field of work. When you bid on a project, the person who listed the gig can view whether you are capable of and right for the task at hand. Not only can they see your portfolio of past work and reviews from happy clients, but now with a skills certification, they can see yet another level of added credibility that will help you stand out from other freelancers.

Personally, when I seek gig workers to help me with a project, I want only the best. I don't want the cheapest worker that is learning the skill as he goes, using my project for practice. I want the one who lives and breathes that line of work—the one who understands every facet of the project, someone who can get it done in the quickest and most efficient manner.

When I hire people, I look at their portfolio, what they've done in the past, their reviews, and their certifications. If they're certified, that puts them above the rest. Their certification tells me that an independent, third-party has verified that they know what they're doing. It shows that the candidate has invested in themselves in order to maintain a high caliber skill set that they can use on my project.

Just as there is a certification for nearly every field of work, there are skills tests for nearly every field as well, from software programs such as Photoshop, InDesign, and Excel, to language skills, grammar, proofreading, and so on. So whether you're in IT or you're a copyeditor, there's likely a test for you.

These qualifications are rather new to the industry, but

they are here to stay. You should expect to see more and more companies looking to certifications and skills tests to narrow down gig workers bidding on their projects. And since the gig economy continues to grow and grow, you can expect a lot of competition, so it's important to obtain the qualifications to help differentiate you from the rest. Again, as I mentioned above, signaling that you're the best fit for the job is key, so adding a skills test to your resume or bio is a great way to signal your competence.

ADOPT A LEARNING MINDSET

In this economy, the most important quality you can have is a beginner's mind. Be humble, ask questions, and assume you'll never know it all because you won't. Something will change, and soon, whether it's the technology and tools you need to master, the gig-company's goals, or the market itself. If you're open to that change, you'll stay in the game. If you're working in the gig economy, continually educating yourself is a must; on average, freelancers train themselves and reskill every four to six months.[19]

Reskilling every four to six months? Sounds hectic and overwhelming. As soon as you get the hang of something, you have to learn something entirely new?

Don't let that discourage you. I think it's a good thing. If you

19   https://www.weforum.org/agenda/2017/07/skill-reskill-prepare-for-future-of-work/.

focus on what you're good at in the first place, this won't be overwhelming. As things change—and technology is always changing—it's important to keep a tab on these changes and grow with them. Sometimes this might mean slight tweaking to your current skill set. Sometimes it might mean something more significant, like a certification or more schooling. But if it's all in the same vein of where your talents lie, you shouldn't feel overwhelmed.

Let me give you a personal example. As a digital marketer, I knew how to get people to a website, and I also knew how to grow the website, but I didn't know how to monetize a site when I first started. It was something I very much needed to know to fill out my skillset and operate a successful business. After all, making money was key to me succeeding after branching out on my own. It took some time researching and learning, but I was able to reskill in my field, which later helped me level up against the competition.

And I'm still learning how to monetize today. I'm constantly learning and expanding my knowledge. This can be done in a number of ways. Sure, you can take a fancy online course, but you can also learn on a micro-level. YouTube and other online tutorials/learning platforms have made it easier than ever to get trained in various skills. If you know nothing about design, you can watch a few videos and gain a decent understanding of the Adobe Creative Suite. Or if you wanted to learn how to make killer marketing videos using your smartphone, you could do that with a little browsing on YouTube. You'd be surprised at the amount of free content you can find there. There are also many free webinars available and plenty of free articles that will pertain to your work or your skills.

Once you've exhausted the free content, you can opt to pay for courses or for platforms like Lynda.com. Do your research to ensure that the ones you pay for offer value. We live in an age where there is virtually unlimited information about any field we are working in, so be sure to take full advantage of that. Go down the rabbit hole and see where it takes you.

Learning new tricks of your trade may take many forms, and unexpected forces can cause you to drop everything to learn how to deal with an issue. For example, when I was building Ridester.com in the early years between 2016-2018, it seemed like whatever I touched on that site turned to gold. Traffic would continue to increase month over month, the affiliate programs were paying out incredible amounts of money, and it seemed like I could do no wrong. Well, one day in June of 2019, my traffic plummeted over 50 percent. In my hubris, I did not see that coming. Somebody had built hundreds of thousands of spam links to my site, effectively launching a negative SEO attack against me. In haste, I dived into how to solve the problem, reading anything I could get my hands on to teach myself how to resolve this issue. After doing what seemed like nothing but reading for weeks on end, I eventually reversed the damage, disavowed the links, and my site started seeing the traffic numbers from before—but this took four months to work through. It was an important lesson of checking egos at the door and adopting that forever learning mindset. If you think you've learned it all, one mistake can have drastic consequences that can very well cripple you and your gig.

I'm not advocating that you try to be an expert in everything across multiple industries. I'm advocating that you focus on your area of expertise and look to be the best you can be in that field. There's always something to be learned.

WARNING: BEWARE OF SCAMMERS

In your quest to feed your learning mindset, beware! There are tons of predatory people on the internet. They want to take advantage of people looking to make money. There are tons of companies that offer training courses and certifications, but a lot of them are complete bullshit. But to someone who's just entering the gig economy, you might not know any better. Do not get conned. Before you pay for any course online, look to see if the same material is offered for free. I'm willing to bet that it is.

Watch out for companies that display a timer on their website, claiming you only have a certain amount of time to secure the deal listed on the product's landing page. That's a marketing tactic to encourage people to impulse buy when it's really not necessary. I'd also be wary of any course that is not refundable. Most legitimate people that offer a product of actual value will understand the value outweighs the price, so they'll offer a refund within a certain timeframe. If they don't, move on.

I speak from experience. I spent way too much money on courses and learning materials when I was first starting out. If I were to do it over again, I'd be more tactical about my approach. Don't get caught up in the hype and the excitement of new courses or products because you can lose a lot of money and waste a lot of time. Be sure to do your research before paying. I once paid $499 for a course and walked away with no new knowledge. I had seen the same content on YouTube for free. Later on, with a lesson learned the hard way under my belt, I did my research regarding a course given by an industry leader in website design, and it was well worth the $1,200. The course ended up having loads of content that I had never seen anywhere else, and I learned a ton from that course.

Tip: As you start out, learn all you can without paying for education. Once you've exhausted the free information and you find yourself reading the same stuff over and over again, consider making the jump into paid educational resources. But do your research before you pay.

You can also Google search the company's name to see what pops up. People love to share their experiences, both good and bad, so check online communities like Reddit. Also, check out the company's social media platforms and read comments from people who have already taken the training or used the product or service in the past. You can get a good sense of whether a company is legit based on people's reactions. If the comments are turned off, that's a red flag.

Even if you're careful and you do the appropriate amount of research, you still might fall victim to getting scammed. I was scammed out of $12,000 from a seller on Flippa, an online marketplace that facilitates the buying and selling of online businesses. I found a website on the site that had a high domain authority and a lot of traffic, which are two things that are hugely important when purchasing an existing website.

The seller was very communicative and clear; it seemed like he knew exactly what he was talking about. By all rights, things seemed to add up, so I bought the site. After the purchase, however, I realized the seller had used bots to inflate the traffic numbers on the site, and the attractive domain authority came from him purchasing an expired domain and putting a new site on that domain. When I tried calling to confront him, the phone number that had previously worked was dead. He used a burner number that he deleted once the transaction went through. And because

I used Flippa's "Buy Now" payment option via PayPal, I couldn't get the money back because it was instantly available to the seller and wasn't escrowed.

Mind you, this was at a point where I knew what I was doing, too. I wasn't some ignorant first-timer. Unfortunately, scammers can be savvy, and they definitely know how to sucker you in. It can happen to anyone. If it happens to you, try not to dwell on it or feel bad about yourself. Learn from the experience—like to never use PayPal for a transaction like this—count your blessings and move on.

STAY ON TOP OF UPDATES

It should go without saying, but whatever you excel in, wherever your skills lie, stay on top of them. This will vary from field to field, but be sure to be alert to any updates or offerings in your industry, paying particular attention to updates related to technology.

This is different than reskilling in order to gain new skills in your field. For example, if you work with Photoshop, you have to be on top of any changes to the program itself. If Adobe, which owns Photoshop, pushes an update, and you're bidding on a project that requires you to use the software, but you don't know how to do whatever it is that they just pushed in the update, you're now at risk of falling behind the competition who might be bidding against you.

If you work for an app-based platform, you have to pay attention to their updates and new features as well. For instance, Uber recently introduced a "quiet mode" option for customers. If a rider is looking for a ride but isn't in the mood to talk to the driver, they can now indicate that they'd prefer to sit in silence. If the rider chooses that option, they expect the driver to quietly drive them to their destination. If the driver didn't pay attention and didn't get the update, they might engage in conversation and get a bad rating, which then affects the number of Uber clients they receive in the future.

CHARGE WHAT YOU'RE WORTH

When I initially took on clients, I didn't really know what I was doing. When I was making websites for people, I would bid on projects on the cheap. On one bid, I wrote out what I was going to do, how long it was going to take, and my price: $500. It was going to be a seven-page website, with three rounds of revisions included in the bid. The client agreed, but during the process of working together, they kept asking for more and more. Can you design my logo? Can you add another page? Can we add a video to the homepage? The list of last-minute requests went on and on.

It got so bad that at one point, I asked myself why I was even doing the project. I was not having fun. The lesson: the cheaper you price your work, the more they'll take. This particular project ended up costing me money rather than putting money in my pocket.

I decided to charge more just to see what would happen. I started charging fair market rates—thousands of dollars instead of hundreds—and I was delighted by the results. Not only did I find clients who didn't bat an eye at the price tag, but these clients were much easier to work with. They knew what they wanted, they communicated well, and they understood that they needed to pay for quality work.

The same principle applied to the content I built at Ridester. com. I invested in buying an online course that was created for rideshare drivers. It covered the ins and outs of starting out as a driver, how to get paid, how to maximize your time behind the wheel, and so on. My intention was to add value to the users on the site and offer the entire course for free. I thought thousands of people would sign up, but to my surprise, not many did. It wasn't until I charged $400 for the course that people started to sign up.

It's contradictory to what you would probably think, but if something's free, people think there's minimal value in it. But if they're going to pay a hefty price, like $400 in my case, then they automatically denote a value. The same applies to clients that are bidding on freelance work. When it comes to bidding on projects, don't undervalue yourself, your time, and your work. It wasn't until I raised my prices that people took me seriously and treated me right.

This will also help you avoid taking clients that will drain you of time and patience for very little money in return. Charge more than you think you're worth, and you won't get people who take advantage of you. Instead, you'll likely get clients that understand that they are paying for quality and appreciate the quality work you do in return.

Tip: Guard your time. It's the most valuable asset you have. Protect it. It's how you make money. For context, I don't take meetings unless it makes sense to do so. I recently took a call from a lady whose company offered a health insurance and benefits package for gig workers. After a brief initial email exchange, I decided to get on a call because it seemed that I could promote her product on Gigworker.com. However, the call ended up being a total waste of my time. Before getting on the phone, I specifically told her I was only interested in one aspect of the insurance, but instead, she tried to sell me on something entirely different during the call. It was the classic bait and switch. Even worse, when I told her I wasn't interested, she began yelling at me and trying to convince me otherwise. Unfortunately, there's a lot of people out there that are not worth your time, so be wary of them. Before taking any meeting or phone call, I ask if the person requesting the meeting or call would mind first outlining everything in a brief email. I know that I can typically handle almost everything through email, but if it makes sense to get on a call, then we do that—but only after we try to handle the issue over email first. The funny thing is that this trick works most of the time. I'm rarely in meetings or on phone calls. Nearly everything gets solved via email, saving me an enormous amount of valuable time that I can use to do something else.

MAKE DECISIONS DELIBERATELY

Every decision you make directly affects your earning potential, so think things through before you do them. It's tempting to make emotional decisions in the heat of the moment in this fast-moving field. Many people get frustrated by challenges on the job and give up prematurely or hop from gig to gig. It's fine to make big moves, but first, evaluate the pros and cons of the situation. If it's truly an unhealthy relationship, you don't have to stay, but be deliberate about your decisions.

This covers a wide spectrum of things—and I don't just mean the obvious things related to your business. We mentioned earlier conducting a cost-benefit analysis of potential earnings with each gig, but have you applied that same concept to things like cleaning your house? How much time does it take to clean your house? How much money could you make in that time? Is it worth it to hire someone to clean your house, or to instead do it yourself? Calculating the hourly rate you can make working in the gig economy, then benchmarking tedious activities against that offers surprising results that can potentially increase your income.

I don't clean my house because it takes too much time. I could instead be spending that time making money. I'd rather pay someone $150 to come to my house twice a month because I'm confident I could make more working on my business in the same amount of time. On the other hand, I cut my own grass. I happen to have purchased a zero-turn lawnmower from an online agricultural equipment wholesaler on Cyber Monday a few years back. I got the mower at a 60 percent discount because it had a big dent in the side. But, since it's a lawnmower, I didn't care since I would probably (and definitely have) beat the living hell out of the thing anyway myself. That beautiful machine gets the job done in ten minutes or less, so it doesn't make any sense to pay someone to mow for me.

Making decisions deliberately boils down to being as efficient as possible. Schedule your days and block out time to tackle your do-to list. There's a book called *Deep Work: Rules for Focused Success in a Distracted World* by Cal Newport, which I highly recommend.

The crux of the book is that there are two kinds of work we do: deep work and shallow work. Deep work is rare and hard—things that demand a high level of concentration. Shallow work is easy and ubiquitous—things we do on auto-pilot, like replying to emails or engaging with others on social media accounts. It recommends blocking a certain amount of time for the shallow work, whether that's an hour twice a day or half an hour in the morning. Once that block of time has passed, you stop doing the shallow work and move onto the deep work. That way, your mind stays sharp for the deep work, and you're not wasting precious energy on the shallow stuff.

When I'm at my office, I oftentimes purposely leave my phone in my car, so I'm not distracted during periods of deep work. I also limit my social media use to one hour per day using distraction-blocking apps and Chrome plugins. Getting constant texts, calls, and notifications steals my time away from the things I need to accomplish. This is why I don't even bother with some social media apps. When Snapchat first came out, for instance, I downloaded it and then deleted it an hour later. During that hour, I kept getting

Snaps from friends. Given that they were just sending me pictures of themselves at work, no less, using the app was a horrendous waste of my time. I deleted the app and haven't downloaded it since.

Bottom line: Since distraction is the enemy of productivity, making deliberate decisions will help you maximize your earning potential in whatever field you're working in.

UNDERSTAND THE GIG

You must take the time to know exactly how the gig is supposed to work. This sounds basic, but you'd be surprised how often people skip this step. Driving for Uber isn't as straightforward as it might seem because not every hour of the day has the same value. If you don't know that, you can easily work six to eight hours per day—the slow hours—and make very little money. If you switch your hours to the optimal shift, however, you'll see a big difference. But you won't know that unless you do a little research.

If you have a rental on Airbnb, you can outsource the property management completely, significantly limiting the amount of time you need to spend managing and booking clients. Obviously, these rental companies take a cut of roughly between 8 to 10 percent of each booking, but that could be worth it if you don't want to manage the listing yourself or have better things to do with your time. It really boils down to what your time is worth. Again, if you can make more money outsourcing a task, then outsource it.

If you don't want to lose 8 to 10 percent of each booking, there are a variety of hacks you can implement to streamline the amount of work surrounding your rental. Instead of meeting your guests at the house to give them your key, install a lockbox on the door, and share the code during booking. That way, you don't have to take the time to physically greet anyone to give them access to your place.

Incorporate an iPad in the house that welcomes your guests and answers all of their questions. I once met a woman with several rental properties who removed all the TVs from her units because she was spending so much time answering basic questions about them, like how the cable box worked, even though there were clear instructions given to guests during arrival. After one too many late-night calls complaining about the TV not working in some way or another, she decided to simply eliminate the problem altogether—no more TVs. Since everyone nowadays has a smartphone with access to virtually unlimited entertainment, her move was pretty brilliant in understanding what she could do in order to make her life a little smoother.

People tend to thrive in environments in which they're most comfortable, which then gives them tunnel vision and keeps them from maximizing their earning potential.

Take Rover, for example. A common mistake Rover workers make is pigeonholing themselves to one aspect of the job—either dog sitting or dog walking. Someone may only choose dog walking because they better understand what that involves compared to dog sitting. It's what they're comfortable with because it's what they know. What they fail to realize, however, is that they could make ten times more money by dog sitting *and* keeping the dog overnight. Sure, there are other things to consider since the gig's responsibilities change, but once the gig worker understands those changes, they can open themselves up to earning more with less time, less energy, and less effort.

Tip: One advantage of an app-based platform versus freelance is the way you get paid. When you drive for Uber, deliver through Postmates, or babysit through SitterCity, the app works as the brokerage and pays out once you complete your work. When you freelance, you have to invoice your customer, wait to get paid, and if it comes down to it, try to collect your money. Sometimes people don't pay for months, even years. So things have the potential to get ugly.

Another key thing to understand when it comes to gig work is the majority of it is review-based, meaning people will publicly judge you on your past work and the feedback you've previously received. This rating system is built into most, if not all, app-based gigs because it works as a sort of checks and balances in weeding out poor workers and customers. On top of the skills that are required for your gig of choice, your customer service skills should also be a huge priority so you can earn positive reviews and increase your probability of getting more work.

Every gig has its quirks, so be sure to talk to others to discover what experience has taught them. Chances are that any problem you're facing is not new; your colleagues can provide valuable information and support.

Through Ridester, for example, the most common question I see is, "Is the gig work related to rideshare driving worth doing?" Unfortunately, I cannot answer that question for you. You need to evaluate yourself, your skills, and how you work to determine if you'd be a good fit for the gig. And since each gig has its own quirks, you need to research for yourself to answer that question. Revisit Chapter Four to see if the gig economy is right for you.

A good place to start is Gigworker.com, but by no means is that the only place. If you're interested in an app-based gig, check out forums online where workers share their successes and failures. Visit Reddit to see if anyone has shared their insight. There are several sources out there for you to explore, so you have a solid understanding of the job before you even start.

POWER OF NETWORKING

When it comes to freelancing or consulting, don't forget to network. Join your local chamber of commerce, or join a charity organization. Not only is this a great way to meet potential clients for your business and bring awareness to what you're doing, but it's always great to get involved in your community. In addition to local, face-to-face networking, be sure to check out online networking opportunities in your field as well. There are countless forums and groups online to engage in. Facebook and LinkedIn are good places to start. I am involved in several groups, and in addition to putting my name out there, I find myself constantly learning from my peers. It's a win-win.

And don't underestimate the power of word of mouth. The more work you do for people, and the more satisfied they are, the more likely they will recommend you to family, friends, and colleagues. Referral traffic in the freelancer world is huge, but it takes time to build the reputation required to get those referrals. You have to build your client base, do quality work, and leave good impressions. Once your reputation is established, not only will you find work less stressful and time-consuming, but the work will start finding you.

This doesn't really apply to app-based gig platforms; instead, it's important to keep your readiness as high as possible, so you get assigned work. You're still motivated to do a good job, however, for positive reviews and higher tips.

SUCCESS STORY: HOW JILLIAN GOT IN

My friend Jillian slowly but successfully eased herself into the gig economy, despite having some initial fears.

She was working full-time as a Brand Manager for a restaurant group that included several food concepts. Jillian was in charge of their marketing strategy, email campaigns, website management, social media content, and brand reputation. She also assisted with some graphic design and photography.

One day while we were at lunch, she brought up the topic of entering the gig economy. We had a conversation about her being inspired by what I was doing, but she said she was anxious to venture out on her own.

"Why is that?" I asked her.

"Well, I'm struggling with not knowing what my income would look like. Right now, my definition of success is a paycheck every two weeks. I think I need a mindset shift."

"That's fair," I said. "What are you looking to get out of it?"

Her corporate marketing job had stability, set hours, and a steady paycheck. But she knew she was created for more. She wanted to pursue her passion wholeheartedly and see what could happen when she put all of her efforts into turning her side-hustle into a full-time career.

"What if you start slowly, Jill?" I said to her. "Why don't you work a few hours a week on whatever it is you really want to do?"

The idea of a flexible schedule, working from home, and bringing her longtime ideas to life was exactly what she dreamed of. She had a successful graphic design business and lifestyle blog that were both growing faster than she could keep up with. Her nights and weekends were dedicated to packing and shipping orders from her Etsy shop, where she sold greeting cards, journals, and prints.

I suggested that she needed to do some additional research before making the plunge. She needed to scope out the market and see what people in the space were looking for. What were they willing to pay? She needed to do a cost analysis. She also needed to learn to stand out from the competition.

Her company, The Anastasia Co (theanastasiaco.com), had a pretty sizable following at the time, so she really leaned into what it was her ideal client was looking for. She took time to research and focus on each part of her business to ensure it was the best that it could be, analyzing everything from SEO and product photography to content creation and relationship building.

"You should add a shop to your website and keep your Etsy

shop," I told her. "I'll be here to answer any questions when you get stuck and can help out if you'd like."

And she did. She created her own online store and marketed her work on Pinterest, Instagram, Facebook, and email. She optimized her website, steadily grew her social media following, and increased her online sales while she still held her position at the restaurant group—impressive, if you ask me.

After four years of balancing two jobs, Jillian felt comfortable leaving her corporate marketing job. She successfully eased into full-time gig work because she did all the right things. She did some soul searching and established her mission, then became crystal clear on who her target customer was. It wasn't just about the money. Even though her day job offered stability with a consistent paycheck, she wanted to create something of her own and be able to focus on the things that mattered most.

One year after going out on her own, her stepfather became sick. She was able to be there to care for him much more than she would have with a traditional job, and having this time with him meant everything to her. It really puts life into perspective. She always says that life is too short to live only for the weekend, and she encourages people to find something that makes them excited to wake up every single morning—it's possible!

Jillian eased into the gig economy by starting a blog and an Etsy shop. Over time she has created a successful home decor and stationery brand. Her products are currently sold in over 250 shops across the United States and Canada, and several new retailers are added monthly.

She's absolutely killing it, to say the least. She has an incredibly dedicated following, has her finger on the pulse of the market, and continually produces products her clients love. She continues to differentiate herself, too. She's been featured in several publications, podcasts, and interviews, which helps her stand out from the competition. She's truly a gig economy success story, and then some.

HOW JOSH FAILED TO GET IN

Whereas Jill slowly eased in, acknowledged her values, and did her research, another friend of mine jumped into the gig economy without doing the necessary planning.

Needless to say, it didn't work out too well for him.

Josh has shiny-object syndrome. He jumps on gigs very quickly without doing much research, and he's highly motivated by money. (Note: Being motivated by money isn't a bad thing, but it can often blind you to accepting work that you might not be a good fit for because you're chasing that end sum.)

Josh worked for a large publishing company, but when someone out of the blue asked him to design a website for them, he agreed. After he made a few hundred dollars from this one side gig, he immediately wanted to form a company around designing websites.

He put together an LLC and began to recruit clients. He wanted hundreds of clients—before having perfected even one. He put the cart before the horse without fine-tuning the process.

Without doing much research or establishing what his values were to launch himself into working for himself, he founded his company and started spending significant amounts of money on ads in hopes of gaining clients. His ads paid off; he signed on a handful of clients. Josh was proud of himself, but as soon as he started to build their sites, problems arose. His work wasn't that great, and his clients started to complain. With his frustration at an all-time high, instead of dealing with it, he just walked away. As it turned out, he got a bunch of tire kickers who wanted way more than he should have been giving them. Because of this, he ended up shutting that company down because he couldn't make the economics work.

Tire kicker: someone who tries to get a deal even though they're already getting a deal.

FAIL FORWARD

Along those same lines, I have a personal anecdote from another failed business venture I was involved with. After eventually seeing success in the gig economy, I jumped right onto the next big thing—selling magnetic baby locks. I was approached by a friend who had the idea to manufacture and sell magnetic locks that would go on cabinets to keep babies and toddlers from getting into them.

The locks were only one small part of the bigger vision: to create a website for parents answering all of their baby- and toddler-related needs. The friend who approached me proposed a partnership where he would do most of the work, and I would be a passive investor. He would do the actual work, and I would fund the operation, then offer advice, suggestions, and strategy when needed.

I decided to invest in the idea because I saw the long-term potential of making the site a lifestyle brand, meaning one that could have a long customer cycle. The site would offer a lot of information related to babies and parenthood— advice, health and wellness information, and best products. Our magnetic locks would be under the products section, and the long-term plan was to sell other baby products as well. Additionally, we had the intention of introducing even more information and products to upsell our customers as their children grew older.

We created a website, designed the locks, then initiated a manufacturing run in China. Everything about the project started looking good. From the branding to the ever-increasing website traffic, to the baby locks themselves, I was happy with our hard work and how everything was turning out.

Well, being that Amazon is an e-commerce juggernaut with many different sellers, others ended up ripping off our magnetic lock design. As a result, my business partner panicked and decided to move the locks from a warehouse in the United States to another cheaper one in Canada.

We had two shipping containers full of these things, but when we moved warehouses, they somehow got lost at the border. They just disappeared. We filed an insurance claim, and even though we got our money back and could have reordered the locks, we were ready to throw in the towel and decided to shut down the company.

I ended up taking it, relieving my business partner of any involvement. In hindsight, we didn't know what we were doing and didn't have an aligned value system and grit to guide us through tough times. If we had spent the time to do a little soul searching and establishing our value system, we could have avoided the time and energy wasted on the baby lock company that didn't work out. If we properly did a little research before going all in, or if my business partner had focused his energy on things he was already good at or had a passion for, we might have been successful.

Because both my business partner from the baby lock venture and Josh lacked passion, they both lost interest in the projects when things got hard. Since they were just chasing the money, when challenges arose, their immediate reaction was to give up. Don't be like those two. When you give up and move onto the next thing instead of pushing forward with what you started, you fail to perfect your skills, and you'll never make a recurring stream of revenue or gain much traction in the gig economy.

I firmly believe that in business, money is simply a byproduct of what you enjoy doing. This advice is somewhat contrary to mainstream advice, which would tell you that if you're looking to make money through what you enjoy doing, you need a business plan and a bunch of structured planning. While I believe a business case should be made for progressing a passion from a hobby to a legitimate business, I don't think a super-strong business case needs to be made beforehand. If you have a passion that has no ability to make money, it's a passion that's a hobby. If you have a passion that you want to make money with, then it can become a business.

But the second it stops being fun, you need to reevaluate what you're doing and make some changes. In the next chapter, I'll share some tips on how to survive the gig economy.

CHAPTER SIX

SURVIVING THE GIG

I've said this before, but I'll say it again: the gig economy is not for everyone (see Chapter Four). Working in the gig economy can be like riding an emotional roller coaster. The high points are fantastic, but you have to endure the lows, too. Everybody does, so when it happens to you, it's just a part of the gig.

Gig work is hard. It's going to toughen you up. You are solely depending on yourself. There's no boss telling you what to do. There's no company looking out for you. There's no consistent paycheck after clocking in the hours. Working alone can be exciting, liberating, and amazing, but it can also be scary, lonely, and stressful.

You'll encounter issues that will put things in perspective. Before, you might be stressing out because you were running late to a meeting. In the gig economy, you'll be stressing out when you lose half of your revenue overnight. But with your commitment to yourself and your values, you will persevere. And when you do, you will look at problems and hardships differently. And in time, these hardships will decrease in scale as you learn to navigate your new waters. You won't understand how strong you are until you've almost failed a hundred times. After a few high-stress hardships, you'll start to look at previous hardships like child's play.

In this chapter, we'll address some of the common obstacles and ways you can overcome them.

AVOID BURNOUT

I know a designer who went out on her own and quickly found herself working fourteen-hour days. She was shocked. She knew she'd be spending a lot of time creating and selling, but she had no idea she'd also be building a social media presence and pursuing other income streams, like affiliate commissions, to support her business.

If this happens to you, you have to become more efficient. Stop selling your time and energy; instead, monetize your efforts and create a machine that will ultimately support product creation. A great example of this is renting a home through Airbnb. Just like rental homeowners hire a property manager to make owning and renting a rental property passive, there are entire companies that have sprung up to make renting property on Airbnb passive as well. For a small amount of money, Airbnb hosts can hire a company to manage bookings, cleanings, and other time-consuming things. In short, you can make money on Airbnb with very little work.

It also helps to talk to others in your industry. Find that forum we talked about in the last chapter where you can vent. When you post, "I'm going nuts with all this work," chances are, you'll get a chorus of "Yeah, me, too" in reply. People love to share how they overcame their struggles; perhaps their stories can help you get through yours.

That kind of support can work wonders, as it did for a guy we'll call Jack, when he became a contractor. Jack had a talent for getting clients, and he did excellent work for them, but in the process of trying to build a safety net, he overcommitted and lost control of his schedule. That's easy to do when you're thinking about the four jobs you have right now, what might go wrong with any one of them, and how you might not get another one for six months. Faced with that uncertainty, you say yes to everything and get overwhelmed.

Jack was working all the time when his worst nightmare came true—a contract he thought was going to make a significant difference in his income pulled out. He lost his footing on the mental tightrope he'd been walking and just bottomed out.

Fortunately, he had people to talk to. He could talk through the problem with someone who understood. My advice? Get down to the bare necessities. Do the things you need to do and ignore everything else, and you'll be fine.

It turned out Jack was more than fine. Losing that contract actually saved him money and eliminated a huge source of stress. It also taught him to stop and think through any commitment, which has made controlling his schedule much easier. He works steady hours now, feels good, and spends more time with friends and family.

PRACTICE SELF-CARE

When you're working your own hours, enjoying what you're doing, and funding the lifestyle you want, people often assume you're trouble-free, but working for yourself can be incredibly demanding. When I first started out, there was so much to learn, and I tried to do it all at once. It wasn't until later that I understood that there was a learning curve that takes time to learn. I didn't have a steady paycheck to fall back on, though, so I was stressed about making ends meet. It was a hard, psychological thing to get over. In fact, it took me a few months.

As time went on, I looked like a success to people looking in from the outside, but they didn't see me on days when I couldn't figure out how to pay the bills or when I was trying to decide what direction to take my projects, knowing full well all of them could implode at any time.

During a particularly stressful year in 2019, I got so stressed and busy that my healthy habits disappeared to the wayside. I ate a ton of fast food because it was so convenient. I didn't work out. And I almost never slept. I gained over ten pounds, rarely had energy, and felt like I was operating at a maximum of 20 percent capacity at any given time.

Additionally, I began battling isolation, loneliness, and depression. As hard as I tried to fight off those feelings, they only continued to get worse. I felt like I was becoming a hollow shell of who I used to be and began to question my decision of leaving that full-time job to do my own thing.

I knew I had to implement some changes before I dug myself into a deep, dark hole from which I couldn't return. And I did, which we'll go over now. I started with working outside of my home. I then created a structured morning routine, hired a therapist, and overhauled my diet.

GET OUT OF YOUR HOUSE

Over time, I realized that to counter feelings of isolation

and loneliness, I needed to get out of my house. I started working in coffee shops. I also made it a point to increase my social interaction. That meant either spending more time with my friends and family or getting to know someone new in my network (with no intention of selling them anything, of course).

Although working at coffee shops was fine, I didn't enjoy working from a laptop. I preferred my home set up with three twenty-seven-inch monitors. What can I say? They unlock a level of productivity that one single screen will never be able to compare to. But working from home was challenging, too; I'd get easily distracted. I thus decided to upgrade and find an office to rent—and I must say, it was one of the best decisions I have ever made. The intentionality of going into an office for the specific reason of working does wonders. It offers a clear separation between home and relaxation and work and productivity. At home, I would easily be persuaded to do anything but work, whereas at my office, there are few distractions; I have to work.

Office spaces in Omaha, Nebraska, are incredibly affordable, but renting your own office might not be feasible for you if you live in an expensive city like San Francisco or New York City. If that's the case, I recommend co-working spaces like WeWork. If your city doesn't have WeWork, check to see if they have something similar. Co-working spaces have been popping up all over the country, even in resort towns, inviting locals and visitors alike to use them. They usually offer a monthly membership fee, but you can also rent the use of the space for a day if you're just traveling through.

> **Tip:** Co-working spaces are a great way to make new friends and get that interaction that most gig workers are desperate for. There are usually an abundance of networking events, mixers, or social hours that allow for interaction among members.

CREATE A STRUCTURED MORNING ROUTINE

The biggest self-care initiative that has worked wonders for me happened after I created a structured morning routine. Implementing this structure to my routine made mornings something I looked forward to each day and helped keep me calm since I knew what to expect. Before creating this routine, I would wake up and either get incredibly overwhelmed with the sheer amount of work I had in front of me, or I would get bored. Now—instead of getting up and seeing a ton of emails in my inbox, then freaking out about how I'm going to get through them all— my morning routine gives me a system for how I tackle each day. It's been a hugely beneficial change.

Although it can alter slightly from day to day, this is what my structured morning routine typically looks like:

- 6:42 a.m.: Wake up and make breakfast.
- 7:00 a.m.: Journal and devotion.
- 7:30 a.m.: Read the news.
- 8:00 a.m.: Meditate.
- 8:15 a.m.: Work out, shower, get ready for work.
- 9:45 a.m.: Head into the office, dedicating the first thirty to sixty minutes to emails. I then choose three big tasks I want to work on for the day and work on them. I select three because that's not an overwhelming number, and I know that I can almost always get three done. After the big three, I then work through a list I have with smaller tasks to complete, and I work my way down them in order of importance and/or priority.

Starting my day this way, every day helps me set expectations for the day, which helps me focus. On average, I get between five to eight hours of work done on most days.

Tip: There are hundreds of books and resources out there about meditation, so I'm not going to go into how I do it. However, I will say this: do it. Meditation is one of the only ways I've found to relieve stress and clear my mind. It does the same thing for me as a thirty-mile bike ride or a ten-mile run, but I don't always have the time for those. Meditation, in turn, has helped me train my mind to better focus, not just on my work but also on my emotions that have the potential to distract me during the workday. I cannot recommend it enough.

HIRE A THERAPIST

Another thing that has helped me is seeing a therapist. As a business owner in the gig economy, there aren't a lot of aspects of my work that my friends and family can relate to, which leads to those intense feelings of loneliness and isolation. Most people view me as living my best life ever and that I should never have anything to complain about. But I commonly encounter issues and challenges just like anybody else; except when I try to share them, I find that people brush off my problems, reminding me that I have it so good. It's sort of a false heuristic.

So instead, I hired a therapist—a third party outsider who will listen and give it to me straight. Although my intention when I first started was strictly related to business, I have gotten way more out of seeing a therapist than I initially thought I would. My therapists, over the years, have helped me understand who I am as a person. They've helped me process the events of my life, such as my parents' divorce, my mom passing away, or relationships that ended poorly, and helped me understand how those events have shaped me into the person that I am today. This, in turn, has not only made me a better entrepreneur, but it has made me a better man, son, brother, and friend.

Tip: If you're thinking about seeing a therapist, which I highly recommend, be sure to do your research beforehand. Don't just call up the first person that pops up on a Google search.

Pay particular attention to what the therapist specializes in, as it could influence the type of questions he or she will ask. I once saw a therapist without doing any prior research, and during our sessions, he would ask all types of awkward sexual questions that had nothing to do with my business. I later learned he was a therapist that specialized in sexual addictions. Needless to say, it didn't work out, and I stopped going shortly thereafter. I currently see someone who specializes in dealing with entrepreneurs, which obviously is a much better fit. Learn from my absent-minded mistake. Save yourself the trouble and do your research beforehand.

WATCH WHAT YOU EAT

What you eat can have a huge impact on your energy, productivity, and mood. If you're eating a lot of processed foods that are high in sugar and saturated fat, your quality of work will suffer. You might not even know it because you don't know any better. Foods high in sugar and saturated fat make you sluggish.

When I fully cut processed foods from my diet, the benefits were outstanding—not only in terms of my work life but in every aspect of my life. I tackled more projects with greater ease throughout the day. I worked out harder. I ran faster. My mental clarity has never been sharper. I can't say enough about the changes I've seen. And dropping that weight I gained was an added bonus.

Your diet doesn't have to be complicated. In fact, it shouldn't be complicated. Food is fuel for your body and mind in order for you to do everything you need to do in a day. My diet is fairly simple: fruit, vegetables, starchy carbs, and protein (mostly chicken). I stay away from anything processed, including candy and sugary baked goods. Staying hydrated is also hugely important. I drink my body weight in ounces of water, which helps give my body the energy and vitality I need to accomplish my goals.

The positive effects of a healthy and nutritious diet spill over into everything: mind, body, and spirit. It also vastly improves your sleep. If you can't afford a place to work or a therapist, tackling and controlling your diet is at a minimum, something that is well within everyone's reach.

Independent work is inherently stressful, so take care of yourself. Eat right. Sleep. Create some distance between your work and the rest of your life. Take time off. Really. The work will be there when you come back.

LACK OF REGULATION

The technology exists to do amazing things—get Amazon packages by drone, buy a self-driving car—but regulation is years behind. A Tesla can drive itself on the highway and on most roads, but it can't drive you all the way from one point to another completely autonomously on some streets because of regulations.

On the other hand, gig companies have a reputation for breaking the rules. When Uber first came to Omaha, they were operating outside the law because Uber drivers didn't have the same type of oversight as a taxi company, and that was illegal. The city cracked down, mounting massive sting operations to catch Uber drivers during rides and issue big tickets. Did this stop Uber? No. They simply leveraged a posse of lawyers to argue their way out of it. Many of the drivers, including myself, kept driving. Uber's "do it first, ask forgiveness later" attitude seemed to have worked—Uber rolled into new markets by embracing the gray area, and now they're miles ahead of the companies that played it safe.

This Wild West attitude appeals to the mavericks among us, but others understandably shy away from work that doesn't come with clear legal boundaries. Say you're a catering worker cooking a meal in someone's house while the homeowners purposely share an intimate moment in the next room. What should you do? Or say an underage kid wants an Uber ride on a rainy day—do you say no because it's against the rules and risk a bad rating, or say yes and risk the chance that the kid says you did something untoward during the ride? Say you're an Airbnb host, but you don't approve of rowdy parties; can you tell your guests what to do?

You'll get little guidance from the parent companies here—they write terms of service dictating what you can and cannot do, but let's face it, you're not going to read every word in terms of service. Even if you do, it might surprise you to find out there's a lot of subjectivity baked in—you often are on your own to decide what you think is right and wrong.

I predict that many of these issues will get resolved as the gig economy continues to evolve, but regulators are still playing catch-up at this point. Not long ago, I started a drone-based aerial video production company, but the regulations were so unclear that after a few people hired me, I wasn't sure if I would get into trouble or not.

That was a grave concern of mine, as I had heard that the FAA would fine people like me thousands of dollars for operating that type of business without a commercial drone license. However, I had also heard of them fining consumer hobbyists for simply flying their drones for fun, so I decided to risk it and keep operating that business.

Six months after I made the decision to move forward, rules were put in place, and potential clients felt much more comfortable hiring me. Now, getting aerial footage is as easy as purchasing a $150 drone from the internet and getting the footage yourself. While I'm glad I took advantage of the opportunity while it was still lucrative, had I waited around for regulations to catch up to innovation, I would've missed out on income. And that's the key here. Don't treat regulations like the Wild West, but when there is an opportunity, reward sometimes outweighs the risk.

Right now, there's no one set of rules that everyone follows, and many gig companies know how to skirt the law, so do your research, find out where you personally stand, and decide for yourself what you are willing or not willing to do. Gigworker.com's future includes advocacy; we plan to use our collective power to encourage pro-gig regulation.

LACK OF BENEFITS AND SERVICES

All the perks you're used to getting at a full-time job—health benefits, life insurance, disability benefits, vacation days, paid holidays, and sick days—are not readily available to the gig worker. It's a crazy state of affairs because gig workers need some of these things more than anyone. Say you're cooking food in someone's home, and you start a fire. No liability insurance? Ouch. Or what if you're delivering a package and you fall down and break a leg. No disability insurance? Now what?

Young people may not mind the lack of benefits as much as older workers; they're more willing to take risks, they don't have a lot of illnesses, and many of them are still covered by their parents' health insurance. Mid-career folks, though, are understandably concerned about losing the benefits they've always had, benefits that their families depend on as well. As they get older, that concern only increases.

Tip: Banks prefer steady paychecks. When I wanted to buy a house in 2015, it was hard for me to get a mortgage despite the fact that I was making more money than I had with a full-time job. The banks denied my mortgage application because I was seen as too "high-risk" for them. The bank saw my business as something that could go under at any time, but they didn't see that if I had a full-time job at a corporation, I could get fired at any time, too. Isn't that the same? It didn't make sense to me.

We need to put together a package program so people can cover these gaps, because there's no robust resource available right now. I would eventually like help in developing one, though, focusing on helping people find the benefits and services they need. My hope is to eventually work toward a solution that works for both parties. I would like to see more protections, but I don't want to see gig companies do more for their contractors, per se. It would be great to see the availability of optional benefits that contractors could purchase. At the same time, that freedom and flexibility that you get come with additional responsibility on your own.

Personally, the flexibility and freedom far outweigh any benefit that I could get at a W-2 job.

In the gig economy, you can make more money, which then allows you to afford health insurance, or even open up an IRA and contribute to that every year. I'd rather take a pay cut to be able to do what I want with my time than to make a little more and then be a slave to a nine-to-five job. Personally, if I made $15,000 less than I would working at a full-time job, I would simply adjust my life expenses accordingly so that I could still freely travel whenever I wanted.

INCOME UNPREDICTABILITY

As a gig worker, your pay isn't capped like it is at a traditional job, so you can potentially earn a lot more. On the other hand, you can't count on getting a paycheck each Friday. Every week, you either make it, or you don't.

Income unpredictability is a problem that sends some people running back to the safety of their corporate jobs, but it is manageable if you plan for it. Go slow. Build a cushion, and remember you'll have more taxes to pay now. Don't leave your full-time job making $50,000 and start driving for Uber if you don't know how you're going to pay the mortgage next month.

Paradoxically, the fix for this is to not focus on the money because the economics change all the time—sometimes overnight. You must be doing this for reasons other than the money—work-life balance, a job you enjoy, a job that makes sense for you—because if you follow the money, you'll be on an endless wild-goose chase.

INDUSTRY CHANGES ARE COMING

One of the benefits for companies in hiring gig workers is that they don't have to follow the strict laws surrounding the treatment of full-time employees. This is currently changing in some states, like California, with their AB5 law, but there are still a lot of unknowns.

HR hasn't had to play a huge role in hiring contract workers. For example, Uber's business is modeled on low-skilled labor with a high number of transactions. Driving is not that hard. So from Uber's point of view, as long as they have a safe driver who's okay, that's good enough to get them on the road. If the driver does a bad job, then the rating system will filter them out, and Uber will then find another driver to replace them. The same cannot be said for a company that contracted with a higher-skilled, professional service—like a software developer. That worker is much harder to attract and retain.

Uber doesn't even look at drivers as an HR issue. They don't call getting more drivers recruitment; they call it acquiring "supply," so they've commoditized human beings in that role. This was part of the reason that California passed its

AB5 bill. It's trying to reclassify contractors as employees if they are needed to do the basic function of the business. Uber could not succeed without its vast network of drivers, so under the new bill, they should be considered full-time employees with benefits. Uber, Lyft, and other gig companies initially pledged $97 million to lobby against the bill but as of October 2020, have actually spent $185 million. As of this publishing, it still remains to be seen how this classification battle will eventually play out.

We'll be keeping tabs on the bill, along with any other gig economy-related bills, at Gigworker.com, so visit us there to stay informed on timely developments.

CONCLUSION

We're on the forefront of another economic evolution, the high-tech version of the Industrial Revolution. When the Industrial Revolution hit, we created new things like skyscrapers, cars, and infrastructure. We also created experts—people who handled one piece of production and got really good at it. New technology arriving on the scene today does the same thing for people and services. Gig workers are the new experts.

I expect many more companies will get involved in the gig economy in the near future, especially with what happened with COVID-19. As companies put even more focus on outsourcing labor, there will be a huge shift in how people, companies, and workers view "doing business." If a company can pay somebody $500 to complete a graphic design project, they probably don't need to hire a full-time designer with a yearly salary and benefits. With that, businesses will become more efficient and cost-effective; fewer people on staff means lower overhead.

Workers will realize they have other options and that a "full-time job" doesn't have to mean a forty-hour workweek. If they become disenchanted with their traditional jobs, they can quit and do something else, something that allows them some freedom to enjoy life.

And they're easy to hire, too. Within only a couple of minutes, I can find a potential hire all the way across the world, have a video call with them, and get them started on my project. I'll look for someone who has done the work before, needs little input from me, and does an excellent job. The process is extremely efficient.

Some may worry that we're taking efficiency too far. Will we eventually take humans out of the equation? Consider the dilemma of an employer in Seattle who has to pay a minimum wage of fifteen dollars per hour for cashiers. Instead of paying high wages to all hourly employees, doesn't it make more sense to just automate that job with a kiosk? Well, maybe. It depends on many factors. Humans won't always be doing the work they do today, but they'll complement computers with insights only humans can have. Maybe instead of hiring several cashiers, the Seattle employer adds two kiosks and hires one host or hostess. Now that person can dedicate time and energy to helping people face-to-face, doing the things only humans can do, while the automated systems focus on transactional efficiency.

Certainly, something will get lost in the new economy. Relationships may suffer because as we commoditize people, we can begin to dehumanize each other. I see it already—how many times have you gotten in an Uber and didn't want to talk to the driver, quietly sitting in the back seat until the end of the ride? It's easy to forget there's an actual human just like you driving the car.

On the other hand, the better and more seamless our interactions with technology become, the more time we have to pursue relationships outside of work and day-to-day transactions.

THE EVOLUTION OF THE EVOLUTION

We are on the cusp of an even bigger evolution: the evolution of the evolution. We already see signs, such as the dramatic rise in venture-capital funding for on-demand platforms: $57 million in 2010 grew to more than $4 billion in 2014.[20]

With all of this investment, we'll soon transition to a much more systemized and efficient environment because ultimately, technology is here to make humans more efficient and drive down costs. The gig economy will evolve like

---

20 https://www.cbinsights.com/research/uber-x-industry-report-2014/.

any other business—why would you hammer every nail by hand to build a house when you could be the person with the nail gun?

Some workers may feel threatened by the advances in technology, but the ones who succeed will be the ones who embrace it and learn to work with it. If an algorithm or a piece of software does something better than a human, that human isn't out of a job. That human has a new job: harnessing that efficiency and using it to grow a business.

As the gig economy matures, we have to be sure to use that efficiency in the right way. One positive trend I see is that the gig economy—the sharing economy—has changed consumer habits. Younger generations would rather use Uber than own a car or pay for a streaming music subscription rather than storing physical discs in their homes.

This shifting view of consumption bodes well for the planet. My parents and grandparents collected a lot of stuff. My house, in comparison, is minimalistic. I don't need a ton of stuff; I'd rather spend my income on experiences like a trip abroad. This shift can be transformative—the world doesn't need more stuff.

THE ROLE OF GIGWORKER.COM

I wrote this book and developed Gigworker.com because

people need these resources to get their bearings in the gig economy so they can grow and succeed.

We are still in the process of building Gigworker.com, but with time it will become the most comprehensive resource about the gig economy on the internet. It will contain the world's largest directory of gig services, products, training, and work but also much more than that. We know what it takes to earn a living in this economy, and we're committed to helping you identify your goals and nurture you along the way to reaching them. We hope to simplify the process and ease some of the frustration, ambiguity, and uncertainty so many gig workers face.

Once we complete the platform, after you log in to Gigworker.com and set up a profile, you'll receive personalized recommendations tailored to your needs. If you've indicated an interest in driving for Uber, we'll give you tips from top-earning Uber drivers, for example. If you're interested in design work, those are the jobs you'll see. Then we'll match you with the gig that seems the best for you. Once we match you with the gig, we'll provide you with services, training, education, information, and products—everything you need to excel.

Gigworker.com might be the go-to website for everything related to the gig economy, but our vision is even bigger. We want to be a platform that other platforms live on. And that starts with millions of people using our tools and providing their feedback. Collectively, those voices will be heard.

I know we can do it because I did it with Ridester, which, in spite of its rudimentary design (people used it, so I never dared to change it), still draws millions of visitors every month. We know what works because people love Ridester features like tips about how to earn more money and avenues for contacting companies. We know what doesn't work, too, because we've analyzed other sites. Most of them are too complicated and confusing and packed with poor-quality listings. Gigworker.com wants to do it differently. We want to be simple and adaptive.

To get there, we took a backward approach to development. While most companies publish quickly to try to get an app out there, we decided to grow our content first, let it rank, and get traffic. Then we analyzed that traffic—how were people getting to our site? What did they need? We used that data to find the right kind of information. Most companies only post the usual suspects—the same part-time, temporary jobs posted everywhere—but with Gigworker. com, we took time to learn the field, analyze the data, develop it methodically, and understand the space and the user.

Our long-term vision for Gigworker.com is to be a catalyst of change in the gig economy. Certainly, we'll reflect the latest trends, but we'll also be driving them. By becoming the go-to place for everything gig, we're connecting the gig workers of the gig economy, creating a community that will not only help individuals succeed but will give them a collective voice in this evolution.

I invite you to continue your journey with me there. Visit the site. Browse our articles by category. Engage in our forums to connect with other gig workers. I hope Gigworker.com becomes a helpful resource in reaching your goals of taking more ownership of your work, your time, and your life. I have faith that Gigworker can help you find the freedom and flexibility that you deserve.

See you there!

ACKNOWLEDGMENTS

This book wouldn't be possible without my mom and dad. It wasn't until I got into gig work, branching out on my own to start my own business, that I realized how hard it is to make a living in this world.

My parents tirelessly sacrificed for myself and my family when I was growing up. They gave up a certain lifestyle so that we could live a fun and fulfilling life. My dad worked tirelessly to start his own business and showed a tremendous amount of grit through the ups and downs of entrepreneurship. My mom also showed that same perseverance and grit when she stayed home and selflessly took care of my siblings and me.

As hard as they worked, they rarely missed a game when I was involved in sports, and they were always there for me whenever I needed it. I wouldn't be where I am today without their hard work, selfless sacrifices, and tremendous support. Even when it seemed like I was crazy for leaving my full-time job to jump into the gig economy full time, they stood by my side and offered nothing but the greatest support.

ABOUT THE AUTHOR

BRETT HELLING is an entrepreneur who specializes in building, growing, and maintaining successful websites. He has worked in the rideshare space since 2014, when he left corporate America behind and started driving for Uber and Lyft in Omaha, Nebraska. Because he loves the freedom and flexibility that come with owning a business, he started Gigworker.com, the website that connects workers to in-depth information about the gig economy and guides users through the vast—and growing—variety of opportunities it offers. When he's not overseeing his team of writers and developers, Brett loves to run and spend time with his dog, Baxter.